W9-DEV-885

Confederate Navy
Quizzes and Facts

By

R. Thomas Campbell

BURD STREET PRESS
SHIPPENSBURG, PENNSYLVANIA

This Burd Street Press publication
was printed by
Beidel Printing House, Inc.
63 West Burd Street
Shippensburg, PA 17257-0152 USA

The acid-free paper used in this book meets the guidelines for permanence and durability of the Committee on Production Guidelines for Book Longevity of the Council on Library Resources.

For a complete list of available publications
please write
Burd Street Press
Division of White Mane Publishing Company, Inc.
P.O. Box 152
Shippensburg, PA 17257-0152 USA

Library of Congress Cataloging-in-Publication Data

Campbell, R. Thomas, 1937-
    Confederate Navy quizzes and facts / by R. Thomas Campbell.
        p. cm.
    Includes bibliographical references.
    ISBN 1-57249-236-8 (alk. paper)
    1. Confederate States of America. Navy--Miscellanea. 2. United States--History--Civil War, 1861-1865--Naval operations, Confederate--Miscellanea. 3. Confederate States of America--History, Naval--Miscellanea. I. Title.

E596 .C33 2001
973.7'57--dc21

00-068087

CONTENTS

INTRODUCTION

Who commanded the CSS *Virginia* when she battled the USS *Monitor* in the first ever clash between armored warship? What U.S. warship was sunk by the CSS *Alabama*? Who commanded the CSS *Florida*? Who was the Confederate Navy's purchasing agent in Europe? Who invented the spar torpedo?

These and hundreds of other questions about the Confederate States Navy are asked and answered in the pages that follow. Much has been written about the Confederate armies—their battles and their great and not-so-great leaders. Relatively little, in comparison, has been published concerning Confederate naval forces. This is beginning to change, however, as more and more historians, educators, and just plain "buffs" discover the world of the Confederate Navy. Most of these researchers and readers, when confronted with the facts, are simply astounded at the naval achievements made by the South in four years of horrific war. Hopefully, you, too, whether you are only mildly curious, or a rabid enthusiast of the Confederate Navy, will find what follows surprising, educational, interesting, informative—and just plain fun.

$\mathbb{F}$ORMATION AND $\mathbb{O}$RGANIZATION

1. On what date was the Confederate States Navy formally established?

2. Name the secretary of the Confederate States Navy.

3. A subsequent act passed by Congress on March 16, 1861, provided for four offices within the department. Name two of the four bureaus.

4. This act also provided for one additional organization within the department. Name that organization.

5. After the Confederate government's move to Richmond, Virginia, where was the Department of the Navy located?

6. Who was the chief clerk who assisted the secretary of the navy?

7. What past experience gave Mallory unique qualifications for the duties of naval secretary?

8. Who was the famous naval officer that President Davis dispatched to the North to purchase arms and ammunition?

9. Secretary Mallory was one of only two cabinet members to retain their offices throughout the war. Who was the other?

10. Name two of the several responsibilities of the Office of Orders and Details.

11. Seven naval officers were successively in charge of the Office of Orders and Details during the war. Name at least three of them.

12. Officers of the navy were classified into what three major categories?

13. Commissioned officers eligible for command afloat were known as "sea" or "line" officers. What were the established ranks of these sea officers?

14. Name the ranks established by the Confederate Congress for warranted sea officers.

15. What were the ranks of commissioned officers not eligible for command afloat?

FORMATION AND **O**RGANIZATION (ANSWERS)

1. The Confederate Congress established the Navy Department on February 20, 1861.

2. Stephen R. Mallory. President Davis nominated Mallory, former senator from Florida, to the position on February 25, 1861.

3. Office of Ordnance and Hydrography, Office of Orders and Details, Office of Medicine and Surgery, and Office of Provisions and Clothing.

4. The act of March 16, 1861, established the Confederate States Marine Corps.

5. On the second floor of the Mechanic's Hall located on Ninth Street between Main and Franklin Streets.

6. Chief Clerk Edward M. Tidball.

7. While in the United States Senate, Mallory had been for 10 years on the Naval Affairs Committee, serving much of the time as its chairman.

8. Captain (later Rear Admiral) Raphael Semmes.

9. Postmaster General John H. Reagan.

10. Preparing and issuing all orders and details for service; matters connected with courts-martial and courts of inquiry; other personnel matters as directed by the secretary; equipment including outfits and stores of vessels, rope walks, and the supplies of fuel.

11. Captain Samuel Barron, from June 11, 1861 to July 20, 1861.

    Captain Lawrence L. Rousseau, from August 1, 1861 to August 23, 1861.

    Captain William F. Lynch, from August 23, 1861 to September 1861.

    Captain Franklin Buchanan, from September 24, 1861 to February 24, 1862.

    Captain French Forrest, from March 27, 1862 to March 16, 1863.

    Commander John K. Mitchell, from March 16, 1863 to May 6, 1864.

    Captain S. Smith Lee, from May 6, 1864 to end of war.

12. Commissioned, warrant, and appointed.

13. Admiral, vice admiral, rear admiral, captain, commander, first lieutenant, second lieutenant, and lieutenant for the war.

14. Master, passed midshipman, midshipman, boatswain, gunner, and master's mate.

15. Surgeon, paymaster, chief engineer, naval constructor, passed assistant surgeon, assistant paymaster, and assistant surgeon.

16. What were the ranks of non-sea warrant officers?

17. What ranks normally constituted appointed officers?

18. What was the maximum number of Confederate naval officers on duty at any one time?

19. A captain in the navy was equivalent to what rank in the Confederate Army?

20. What three naval officers also held a commissioned rank in the Confederate Army?

21. Name the two categories into which sailors in the Confederate Navy could be classified?

22. What petty officer was always assigned to the engine room?

23. Another petty officer was the quartermaster. What were his duties?

24. Which ranks of enlisted men were below petty officers?

25. What was the minimum age for enlistment in the Confederate Navy?

26. Were African Americans permitted to enlist in the Confederate Navy?

27. What was the function of the Office of Ordnance and Hydrography?

28. Name two of the three naval officers who were successively in charge of the Office of Ordnance and Hydrography during the war.

29. Who was the Confederate Navy's Inspector of Ordnance?

30. What officer aboard ship had direct charge of all ordnance equipment?

31. Commander John M. Brooke, through experiments, determined the best slant angle for armor plate that would deflect enemy shells, but still provide enough room for the crews to work the guns. What was this angle?

32. What educational institution fell under the auspices of the Office of Ordnance and Hydrography?

33. What was the function of the Office of Provisions and Clothing?

16. First, second, and third assistant engineers, carpenter, and sailmaker.

17. Secretary to the flag officer, captain's clerk, and paymaster's clerk.

18. Returns for April 1864 give 727 officers present and ready for duty. Twenty-six others were listed as on sick leave, awaiting orders, or suspended.

19. Colonel.

20. John Taylor Wood, colonel; Richard L. Page, brigadier general; and Raphael Semmes, brigadier general.

21. Petty officers and seamen.

22. First class fireman.

23. One who attends to a ship's helm, binnacle, and signals.

24. Seaman, ordinary seaman, landsman, fireman second class, coal heaver, and boy.

25. Fourteen. Many lied about their age, and boys as young as 12 and 13 were not uncommon.

26. Yes. Free blacks could enlist with special permission from the Navy Department. Slaves could enlist with their owner's consent. Many blacks served as pilots, firemen, and officers' servants.

27. To design, develop, purchase, produce, test, distribute, and provide for the maintenance of guns, ammunition, ordnance stores, tools, pyrotechnics, and navigation instruments.

28. Captain Duncan N. Ingraham, June 10, 1861 to November 16, 1861; Commander George Minor, December 1861 to March 1863; Commander John M. Brooke, March 1863 to end of war.

29. Commander Archibald B. Fairfax.

30. The gunner.

31. Thirty-eight degrees.

32. The Confederate Naval Academy located aboard the CSS *Patrick Henry* on the James River below Richmond.

33. Procurement, distribution, accounting for the food and clothing of the navy, and the distribution of pay.

34. The navy supplied its own food to the various squadrons scattered throughout the Confederacy. A flour and grist mill, bakery, and meat-packing plant were established in what Southern city?

35. How did officers in the Confederate Navy acquire their uniforms?

36. The Office of Medicine and Surgery was responsible for all purchases of medicine, medical supplies, and the operation of naval hospitals. Who was the Surgeon in Charge who headed this department?

37. Name five of the seven cities where naval hospitals were located.

38. Name the commander of the Confederate States Marine Corps.

39. What was the maximum reported strength at any one time of the Marine Corps?

40. Who was second in command of the Confederate States Marine Corps?

34. Albany, Georgia.

35. Officers were required to supply their own uniforms.

36. Surgeon William A. W. Spotswood was the navy's chief medical officer, and he directed the Office of Medicine and Surgery for the duration of the war.

37. Norfolk, Pensacola, Richmond, Mobile, Charleston, Savannah, and Wilmington.

38. Colonel Lloyd J. Beall. He commanded the Marine Corps throughout the war.

39. There were 571 as of October 31, 1864. Twelve hundred men, however, are shown on the rolls of the Marine Corps at one time or another.

40. Lieutenant Colonel Henry B. Tyler.

**Secretary of the Navy
Stephen R. Mallory**

**Mechanic's Hall
on Ninth Street in
Richmond, home
of the War and
Navy Departments**

Commander Richard L. Page

One of three naval officers to also hold the rank of brigadier general

Scharf: *History of the Confederate States Navy*

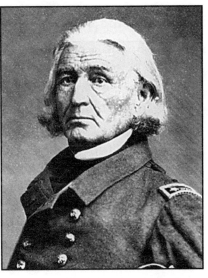

Captain French Forrest

Director of the Office or Orders and Details from March 27, 1862 to March 16, 1863

Author's Collection

Captain Duncan N. Ingraham

First director of the Office of Ordnance and Hydrography

Scharf: *History of the Confederate States Navy*

PRIVATEERS AND CRUISERS

1. What differentiates a privateer from a cruiser?
2. Early in the war the Confederate government issued commissions to individuals who wished to convert their vessels into privateers. What was the name of this commission?
3. Although the United States was not a signatory, what agreement had supposedly abolished privateering?
4. What was the name of the first Confederate privateer to put to sea?
5. What was the date of the first capture of a Northern merchant vessel by a Confederate privateer?
6. Name the commander of the privateer *Calhoun*.
7. Although not a privateer, what vessel was the first to operate in that capacity out of Hatteras Inlet, North Carolina?
8. Name the commander of this first North Carolina warship.
9. Name two other warships of the North Carolina navy.
10. What was the most successful privateer that operated out of Hatteras Inlet, North Carolina?
11. Who was the commander of the Confederate privateer *Gordon*?
12. After her privateering days, what would be the *Gordon's* most memorable claim to fame?
13. What vessel is generally considered to be the most successful of the Confederate privateers?
14. Who commanded this most successful privateer?
15. How many Northern vessels did she capture?
16. What Confederate privateer was sunk by a U.S. warship?
17. The *Sumter* was the Confederacy's first commissioned cruiser. From what port did she sail?
18. Who was the commander of the first Confederate cruiser?
19. How many Northern merchant vessels were captured by the CSS *Sumter*?

$\mathbb{P}$RIVATEERS AND $\mathbb{C}$RUISERS (ANSWERS)

1. A privateer was a privately owned vessel crewed by civilians, but with a commission issued by the Confederate government allowing them to attack and capture Northern merchant vessels. A cruiser was a government-owned and -commissioned warship crewed by regular naval personnel.

2. A letter of Marque and Reprisal.

3. The Treaty of Paris. It was signed March 30, 1856, by Great Britain, France, Austria, Prussia, Russia, Sardinia, and Turkey. Because the United States had refused to sign, the Confederate States felt it, too, was not bound by the treaty.

4. C.S. Privateer *Calhoun*, a 508-ton side-wheel steamer out of New Orleans.

5. May 16, 1861. The *Calhoun* captured the *Ocean Eagle* in the Gulf of Mexico.

6. Captain John Wilson.

7. The NCS *Winslow*, a side-wheel steamer mounting two guns, had been commissioned by the North Carolina navy.

8. Lieutenant Commander Thomas M. Crossan.

9. The NCS *Raleigh* and the NCS *Beaufort*. All North Carolina and most other Southern state vessels were transferred to the Confederate Navy by August of 1861.

10. The C.S. Privateer *Gordan*. The *Gordan* was a 519-ton steamer with a crew of 50 men and carrying three heavy guns. She had originally sailed from Charleston, South Carolina.

11. Captain Thomas J. Lockwood.

12. Renamed the *Theodora*, she carried the Confederate emissaries James M. Mason and John Slidell out of Charleston to the West Indies.

13. The C.S. Privateer *Jeff Davis*, a 230-ton sailing brig out of Charleston, South Carolina.

14. Captain Louis M. Coxetter.

15. Eight Northern merchantmen.

16. The C.S. Privateer *Petrel*. She was sunk by the USS *St. Lawrence* on July 28, 1861, off the coast of South Carolina. Four crewmen drowned and 36 were taken prisoner.

17. New Orleans. The *Sumter* sailed on June 30, 1861, to attack Northern commerce.

18. Captain Raphael Semmes.

19. The *Sumter* captured 18 vessels, seven of which were destroyed and the rest being bonded and released.

20. Who was the executive officer of the CSS *Sumter*?

21. The brother-in-law of President Jefferson Davis shipped as the marine officer on board the *Sumter*. What was his name?

22. Captain Raphael Semmes originally hailed from what state?

23. What was the ultimate fate of the CSS *Sumter*?

24. What was the CSS *Nashville*'s claim to fame?

25. What was the top speed of the side-wheel steamer *Nashville*?

26. From what port did the *Nashville* depart on her historic voyage to England?

27. Who was the commander of the CSS *Nashville*?

28. The *Nashville* created a sensation when she arrived in England representing the new Southern nation. In what English port did she drop her anchor?

29. Who was the executive officer of the CSS *Nashville* on her cruise to England?

30. Upon the *Nashville*'s return from England, what Confederate port did she manage to enter?

31. What was the ultimate fate of the CSS *Nashville*?

32. At a distance, what was the most identifiable feature of the CSS *Florida*?

33. Where was the *Florida* built?

34. To thwart Union intelligence, what dockyard name was given to the *Florida* during her construction?

35. Name the Confederate naval officer who was responsible for the construction of the cruiser *Florida*.

36. When did the *Florida* first set sail?

37. When the *Florida* arrived at Nassau, Bahamas, what Confederate officer took over as her new commander?

38. What was the armament of the Confederacy's first European-built cruiser?

39. What was the fastest speed ever recorded by the *Florida*?

40. The *Florida* participated in two separate cruises against United States commerce during the course of her career. In the first cruise, how many Northern merchant vessels were captured?

20. First Lieutenant John McIntosh Kell.

21. Lieutenant Becket K. Howell.

22. Maryland. Semmes was residing in Alabama at the outbreak of the war.

23. The *Sumter* was sold at auction. Her new owners renamed her *Gibraltar* and converted her into a blockade runner.

24. She was the first warship to display the Confederate flag in the English Channel.

25. The 1,221-ton steamer could make in excess of 16.5 knots.

26. Charleston, South Carolina. The *Nashville* slipped out on the night of October 26, 1861.

27. Lieutenant Robert P. Pegram.

28. The *Nashville* arrived in Southampton, England, on November 21, 1861.

29. First Lieutenant Charles M. Fauntlereoy.

30. Beaufort, North Carolina. The *Nashville* entered the harbor on February 28, 1862.

31. She was destroyed by Union gunfire at Savannah, Georgia, on February 28, 1863. Renamed the *Thomas L Wagg*, and later the *Rattlesnake*, she served as a blockade runner until destroyed.

32. She had two smokestacks forward of the main mast.

33. The *Florida* was constructed at Liverpool, England. Built at the shipyard of William C. Miller and Sons, she was the Confederacy's first foreign-built commerce raider.

34. The *Florida* was called *Oreto* during her construction.

35. Commander James D. Bulloch.

36. March 22, 1862, from England.

37. Commander John Newland Maffitt. A noted blockade runner captain, he arrived in Nassau in early May of 1862. As ranking Confederate naval officer, he immediately assumed command of the *Florida*.

38. Two 7-inch Blakely rifles mounted on pivots, and six 32-pounders mounted in broadside.

39. 14.5 knots on her dash out of Mobile, Alabama.

40. Twenty-four. Of these, 19 were burned and five released on bond.

41. What was the name of the *Florida*'s first executive officer who died from yellow fever?

42. Name one of two reasons why Maffitt ran the gauntlet of Union warships to bring the *Florida* into Mobile, Alabama?

43. Who was the Union commander on blockade duty who desperately tried to stop Maffitt and the *Florida* from sailing into Mobile?

44. After refitting, when did the *Florida* leave Mobile?

45. Who took Stribling's place as executive officer?

46. After more than seven months at sea, where did the first cruise of the *Florida* finally end?

47. After repairs and refitting, the *Florida* went to sea again. Who was her new commander?

48. From what state did the *Florida*'s new commander hail?

49. How many Northern merchant vessels were captured on the *Florida*'s second cruise?

50. The second cruise of the *Florida* ended when she entered what South American port?

51. What United States warship was also anchored in this port?

52. In the dark early morning hours of October 7, 1864, in violation of this country's neutrality, what action took place?

53. What was the ultimate fate of the *Florida*?

54. Who was responsible for the Confederate Navy's acquisition of the CSS *Georgia*?

55. In what country was the *Georgia* built?

56. What was her name prior to being acquired by the Confederacy?

57. What was the *Georgia*'s greatest liability?

58. What was the *Georgia*'s armament?

59. Who was the naval officer who was selected to command the *Georgia*?

60. Name the executive officer of the *Georgia*.

61. What was the top speed of the *Georgia* under steam?

62. How many Northern merchant vessels were captured by the *Georgia*?

41. Lieutenant John M. Stribling. He died on September 12, 1862.

42. He needed replacements for his crew, most of whom had succumbed to yellow fever, and he required some vital parts for the *Florida*'s guns.

43. Commander George H. Preble. An old friend of Maffitt's, Preble commanded the USS *Oneida*.

44. January 15, 1863.

45. Lieutenant Samuel W. Averett.

46. At Brest, France. The *Florida*, in very much need of repairs, arrived on August 23, 1863.

47. Lieutenant Charles M. Morris took command of the *Florida* on January 5, 1864.

48. Morris was born in South Carolina, but had been a longtime resident of Georgia.

49. Thirteen.

50. She arrived in Bahia, Brazil, on October 4, 1864.

51. The USS *Waschusett*. The steam sloop, which had arrived only a few days earlier, was commanded by Napoleon Collins.

52. While most of the *Florida*'s crew was ashore, the *Waschusett* rammed the Confederate cruiser and captured her. Collins then towed the Southern vessel out to sea.

53. She sank while in Union hands under suspicious circumstances in Hampton Roads, Virginia, on November 28, 1864.

54. Commander Matthew Fontaine Maury. He was known as the Pathfinder of the Seas for his development of wind and ocean charts.

55. Scotland. She was built in the shipyard of the Denny Brothers at Dumbarton.

56. The *Georgia* was known during her construction as the *Japan*.

57. She had a very limited coal capacity, thus limiting her range under steam.

58. Two 10-pounder Whitworth guns, two 24-pounders, and one 32-pounder Blakely rifle mounted on a forward pivot.

59. Commander William L. Maury, a cousin of Matthew F. Maury.

60. First Lieutenant Robert T. Chapman.

61. The *Georgia* could make only about nine knots under steam alone.

62. Nine.

63. What was the ultimate fate of the CSS *Georgia*?

64. The *Tallahassee* began life as a blockade runner. By what name was she known at that time?

65. Although privately owned, as a blockade runner she was commanded by what Confederate Navy officer?

66. How many trips were made through the Federal blockade?

67. In July of 1864, the vessel was purchased by the Confederate Navy and commissioned as the CSS *Tallahassee*. Who was given her command?

68. Converted into a cruiser at Wilmington, North Carolina, what armament was placed on board the *Tallahassee*?

69. What was unique about the *Tallahassee*'s mode of propulsion?

70. The *Tallahassee* was fast for her day. What was her top speed?

71. As a cruiser, what was the *Tallahassee*'s greatest liability?

72. What happened on the *Tallahassee*'s first and second attempt at going to sea?

73. The *Tallahassee* finally sailed from Wilmington on August 6, 1864. How many Northern vessels did she capture before her return?

74. Who was the executive officer of the *Tallahassee*?

75. Geographically, where did the cruise of the *Tallahassee* take her?

76. When a second raid was planned, what new name was given the *Tallahassee* in an attempt to deceive Union intelligence?

77. On her second raid, who was the cruiser's new commander?

78. On her second cruise, the former *Tallahassee* left Wilmington on October 24, 1864, and returned on November 7, 1864. During her time at sea, how many captures were made?

79. After her second cruise, what became of the *Tallahassee*?

80. The *Alabama* was the most successful Confederate commerce raider of the war. Who was responsible for her construction?

81. Where was the *Alabama* built?

82. To circumvent British intelligence, what name was given to the *Alabama* during her construction?

63. She was wrecked on the rocky coast of the Gulf of St. Lawrence in 1867. Prior to her loss, she had been decommissioned and sold on June 1, 1864, to an Englishman who converted her into a merchant vessel.

64. Built at the shipyard of John and William Dudgeon Company near London, England, the vessel was named the *Atlanta* (sometimes spelled *Atalanta*).

65. Lieutenant Michael P. Usina.

66. Eight. Four inbound and four outbound.

67. Commander John Taylor Wood, nephew of President Jefferson Davis.

68. A rifled 32-pounder forward, a 100-pounder rifle amidships, and a heavy Parrott rifle aft.

69. The *Tallahassee* had twin screws. Each was driven by its own steam engine, and both engines could be operated together or separately, enabling the vessel to turn upon her center.

70. Greater than 17 knots.

71. Her limited coal capacity. This restricted her range.

72. She ran aground.

73. Thirty-three. Twenty-seven were destroyed; the rest were bonded and released.

74. First Lieutenant William H. Ward.

75. To Halifax, Nova Scotia. She ran along the East Coast of the United States and then returned safely to Wilmington amid a hail of gunfire from the blockaders on August 25, 1864.

76. CSS *Olustee*.

77. William H. Ward, the *Tallahassee*'s former executive officer, now commanded the newly commissioned *Olustee*.

78. Six.

79. She was converted back into a blockade runner.

80. Commander James D. Bulloch scored his most notable success as the Confederate Navy's purchasing agent when he submitted the design, and contracted for, the construction of the CSS *Alabama*.

81. Liverpool, England—at the John Laird Shipyard on the Mersey River.

82. The *Alabama* was known as *Number 290*.

83. The *Alabama* was the largest cruiser ever built for the Confederacy. What was her length and displacement?

84. What was the *Alabama's* recorded top speed?

85. Operating together, how much horsepower could the *Alabama's* engines produce?

86. What two innovations could transform the *Alabama* into a pure sailing ship?

87. What armament was carried by the *Alabama*?

88. To further confuse British and U.S. officials, what name was given to the *Alabama* upon her launching?

89. In what year was the *Alabama* launched?

90. What was the name of the *Alabama's* supply vessel chartered by Commander Bulloch?

91. When the *Alabama* left England on July 30, 1862, who was in command?

92. What ruse did Bulloch utilize to spirit the *Alabama* out of England?

93. Name the *Alabama's* destination upon her sailing from England.

94. Shortly after the *Alabama* left England, a Confederate naval officer arrived in Liverpool. He was destined to achieve fame as the *Alabama's* commander. Who was he?

95. What steamer did Bulloch charter to deliver the *Alabama's* commander and crew to the rendezvous in the Azores?

96. Who was the executive officer of the *Alabama*?

97. Name the second officer and third officer of the *Alabama*.

98. Name two additional officers of the *Alabama*.

99. What was the name of the younger brother of Commander James D. Bulloch who served on the *Alabama*?

100. Where was the home (city and country) of D. Herbert Liewellyn, surgeon of the *Alabama*?

101. What was unique about David White, the wardroom mess steward?

102. Of what nationality were most of the *Alabama's* crew members?

83. The *Alabama* was 220 feet long and weighed 1,040 tons.

84. Fifteen knots.

85. The *Alabama*'s two horizontal engines were rated at 300 hp apiece, but coupled together they produced close to 1,000 hp.

86. She had a retractable funnel and a lifting propeller.

87. Equipped in the Azores after she left England, the *Alabama* carried a 100-pounder Blakely rifle mounted on a pivot forward, an 8-inch smoothbore abaft the main mast, and six 32-pounders in broadside.

88. *Enrica.*

89. 1862. The *Alabama* was launched on May 15.

90. The *Agrippina.*

91. Matthew J. Butcher, an English captain.

92. Bulloch announced that the *Enrica* (*Alabama*) was making only a trial run.

93. Bulloch had arranged for the *Agrippina* to meet her at Terceira in the Azores.

94. Captain, later Rear Admiral, Raphael Semmes.

95. The *Bahama* carried Bulloch, Semmes, some of his officers, and a number of English sailors to the Azores.

96. First Lieutenant John M. Kell, the same executive officer in which Semmes had developed so much trust while commanding the *Sumter.*

97. Lieutenant Richard F. Armstrong and Lieutenant Joseph D. Wilson.

98. Lieutenant John Low and Lieutenant Arthur Sinclair.

99. Midshipman Irvine S. Bulloch.

100. Witshire, England.

101. David White was a Negro slave. A favorite among the crew, the young man from Delaware was entered on the books as a regular crew member and given the pay that his rank required. White drowned when the *Alabama* went down off Cherbourg, France.

102. English.

103. What nickname did the crew give Raphael Semmes?

104. Where was the *Alabama* at the end of 1862?

105. How many Northern merchant vessels had the *Alabama* captured by the end of 1862?

106. Why did *Semmes* sail the *Alabama* toward Galveston, Texas, in January of 1863?

107. What U.S. vessel fought the *Alabama* off the coast of Galveston, Texas?

108. Who was the Union commander of this vessel?

109. In the ensuing night battle, how long did it take the *Alabama* to defeat this Union warship?

110. How many Union sailors drowned?

111. Where did Semmes take the prisoners from the *Hatteras*?

112. When searching for American merchant ships, where was the *Alabama*'s favorite cruising ground?

113. On May 13, 1863, the *Alabama* arrived in Bahia, Brazil. What other Confederate cruiser arrived in port that night?

114. What other Confederate cruiser was in a Brazilian port at this same time farther up the coast?

115. What sailing bark was commissioned as a Confederate cruiser by Semmes after her capture?

116. At what major British port did the *Alabama* arrive on July 29, 1863?

117. In what other British port was the only known surviving photograph of the *Alabama* taken?

118. During the *Alabama*'s 22 months at sea, how many American vessels had she captured?

119. What French harbor would prove to be the *Alabama*'s last port of call?

120. What U.S. warship also arrived in this French port three days later?

121. Who was the commander of this Union vessel?

122. The *Alabama* steamed out to challenge the Union vessel on what date?

103. Old Beeswax for his handlebar mustache.

104. Las Arcas Island off the Yucatan peninsula.

105. Twenty-six.

106. He had learned, via captured Northern newspapers, that a Federal invasion force was on its way there.

107. The USS *Hatteras.*

108. Lieutenant Homer C. Blake.

109. Thirteen minutes.

110. None. The *Alabama* rescued 17 officers and 101 men.

111. Port Royal, Jamaica.

112. Off the coast of Brazil.

113. The CSS *Georgia.* She was commanded by Semmes' old friend, Lieutenant William L. Maury.

114. The CSS *Florida.* She had put into Pernambuco a few days earlier for coal and supplies.

115. The *Conrad.* Semmes commissioned her the CSS *Tuscaloosa* and placed Lieutenant John Low in command.

116. Cape Town, South Africa.

117. Singapore.

118. Sixty-six. Fifty-two were burned, ten were bonded, one (the USS *Hatteras*) was sunk by gunfire, one was commissioned as a Confederate cruiser (the CSS *Tuscaloosa*), one was sold, and one was released.

119. Cherbourg, France. The *Alabama* arrived on June 11, 1864.

120. The USS *Kearsarge.*

121. Captain John A. Winslow. Ironically, he and Semmes had served together on the USS *Cumberland* during the Mexican War and later on the USS *Raitan* where they shared a cabin together.

122. June 19, 1864, a Sunday.

123. Approximately how many people had gathered on the French shore to watch the ensuing battle?

124. What French warship accompanied the *Alabama* out to the three-mile limit?

125. What was the name of the English vessel that would play such an important role at the end of the battle?

126. In the battle between the *Alabama* and the *Kearsarge*, which vessel opened fire first?

127. Why were many of the *Alabama's* shots ineffective?

128. What one shot from the *Alabama* could have ended the battle?

129. Why did solid shot fail to injure the *Kearsarge*?

130. While the *Alabama* had inflicted some damage on the *Kearsarge*, the Confederate cruiser was badly hit and began to sink. How long had the battle lasted?

131. After her flag was hauled down, why did the *Kearsarge* send five more shells crashing into the sinking *Alabama*?

132. When the *Alabama* went down, how was Raphael Semmes rescued?

133. How many casualties were there among the *Alabama's* crew?

134. What was unique about two of the crew members who lost their lives?

135. What artifact was raised in 1994 from the site of the *Alabama's* sinking?

136. Like the *Tallahassee*, the *Chickamauga* began life as a blockade runner. What was her name as a blockade runner?

137. Where was the *Chickamauga* built?

138. As a blockade runner, how many trips through the Federal blockade did the *Chickamauga* make?

139. Who was placed in command after the *Chickamauga* was converted into a cruiser?

140. What was the *Chickamauga's* armament?

141. From what port did the *Chickamauga* leave on her cruise?

142. During her cruise, how many Northern vessels were captured?

143. What was the ultimate fate of the *Chickamauga*?

123. Approximately 15,000.

124. The ironclad *Couronne*.

125. The English yacht *Deerhound*. Owned and operated by John Lancaster, she would rescue many of the *Alabama*'s crew.

126. The *Kearsarge*.

127. Many of the *Alabama*'s shells failed to explode due to old and contaminated powder.

128. A shot from the forward Blakely crashed into the *Kearsarge*'s sternpost, but failed to explode.

129. The Union vessel had heavy chains draped over the sides which were then boxed in with planks. No one on the *Alabama* had noticed this improvised armor.

130. One hour, twenty minutes.

131. Winslow later admitted that he feared Semmes was trying some type of "ruse."

132. Semmes and his executive officer Kell were both rescued by the English yacht *Deerhound*.

133. Forty-two. Nine were killed and 21 were wounded during the battle. Twelve men drowned when the ship went down.

134. Fireman Andrew Shilland and Cabin Boy David White were both black.

135. The Blakely pivot rifle. It was still loaded.

136. *Edith*.

137. The *Chickamauga*, a sister ship to the *Tallahassee*, was built at the Cubitt Town Yard near London, England.

138. Nine.

139. First Lieutenant John Wilkinson.

140. The *Chickamauga* carried three pivot guns—a 64-pounder amidships, a rifled 12-pounder forward, and a rifled 32-pounder aft.

141. The *Chickamauga* left Wilmington, North Carolina, on the night of October 28, 1864.

142. Seven. This was accomplished in three weeks, after which the *Chickamauga* returned to Wilmington on November 19, 1864.

143. She was burned and scuttled. This took place on the Cape Fear River just below Indian Wells on February 25, 1865.

144. What Confederate naval officer was responsible for the acquisition of the CSS *Shenandoah?*

145. Why was the acquisition of the *Shenandoah* of such paramount importance?

146. What was the *Shenandoah's* name prior to being purchased by the Confederate Navy?

147. Where was she built?

148. On what date was the purchase of the *Shenandoah* concluded?

149. What was the purchase price?

150. In order to thwart suspicion from Union spies, who was placed in command?

151. What was the displacement of the *Shenandoah?*

152. For what purpose was the *Shenandoah* originally designed?

153. When did the *Shenandoah* leave England?

154. When the *Shenandoah* sailed from England, who was the mysterious Confederate officer on board known only as "Mr. Brown"?

155. Where was Captain Corbett instructed to take the *Shenandoah?*

156. Who was selected to command the new Confederate cruiser?

157. Name the nephew of General Robert E. Lee who served on the *Shenandoah.*

158. What was the name of the steamer purchased by Commander Bulloch to transport the *Shenandoah's* men, guns, and equipment to the rendezvous?

159. Name the Confederate officer who commanded this steamer.

160. What was the minimum complement of men needed to sail and man the guns of the *Shenandoah?*

161. What guns constituted the *Shenandoah's* armament?

162. How did the instructions for the *Shenandoah's* cruise differ from other Confederate cruisers?

163. When was the *Shenandoah's* first capture made?

164. When was her last capture?

144. Commander James D. Bulloch, the same officer responsible for the *Florida* and *Alabama*.

145. She was considered a replacement for the sunken *Alabama*.

146. The *Sea King*.

147. Glasgow, Scotland, on the River Clyde.

148. September 30, 1864.

149. £45,000.

150. Peter Corbett, a British merchant captain, and an old friend of Bulloch's.

151. One thousand one hundred sixty tons.

152. A fast British troop transport.

153. The *Shenandoah* (*Sea King*) steamed quietly down the Thames River and out to sea on October 8, 1864.

154. Traveling incognito, the shadowy stranger was the *Shenandoah*'s future executive officer, First Lieutenant William C. Whittle.

155. To the island of Madeira off the northwest coast of Africa.

156. First Lieutenant James I. Waddell.

157. Lieutenant Sidney Smith Lee, Jr.

158. The *Laurel*.

159. Lieutenant John F. Ramsey.

160. One hundred fifty men.

161. Four 8-inch smoothbores, two rifled Whitworth 32-pounders, and two small 12-pounders all mounted in broadside.

162. She was instructed to destroy the North American whaling fleet in the northern Pacific.

163. October 30, 1864.

164. June 28, 1865. Eleven whaling vessels were captured in the Arctic Ocean. Ten were burned and one was released on bond with all the prisoners.

165. What was the total number of vessels captured by the *Shenandoah*?

166. How and when did the *Shenandoah*'s commander receive convincing confirmation that the war was over?

167. After consultation with his officers, where did Waddell decide to take the *Shenandoah*?

168. When did the *Shenandoah* arrive at her final destination?

169. Upon her arrival, the last official flag of the Confederacy was lowered by the *Shenandoah*. Where is that flag today?

165. Thirty-eight.

166. From newspapers and the assurance of the captain of the English bark *Barracouta*, 13 days out of San Francisco. The date was August 2, 1865.

167. Liverpool, England.

168. November 6, 1865. The war had been over for six months.

169. The *Shenandoah*'s flag is on display in the Museum of the Confederacy, Richmond, Virginia.

The *Calhoun*, the first Confederate privateer put to sea

The Confederate cruiser CSS *Alabama*

The Confederate cruiser CSS *Shenandoah*

Naval Historical Center

The Confederate cruiser CSS *Florida*

Naval Historical Center

**Lieutenant Commander
Thomas M. Crossan of the
North Carolina Navy**

Clark: *North Carolina Regiments, 1861–1865*

**Commander
William L. Maury**

Naval Historical Center

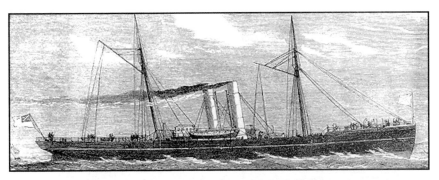

The Confederate cruiser CSS *Tallahassee*

Illustrated London News

The Confederate cruiser CSS *Georgia*

Naval Historical Center

The CSS *Sumter* **running out of New Orleans, June 30, 1861**

Naval Historical Center

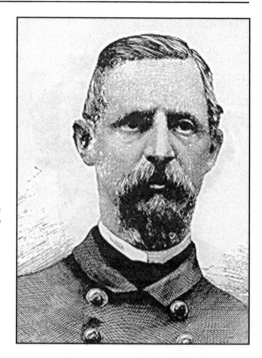

**Lieutenant
Charles M. Morris,
last commander of the
CSS *Florida***

Scharf: *History of the Confederate States
Navy*

**Lieutenant
John Wilkinson,
commander of the CSS
*Chickamauga***

Naval Historical Center

The CSS *Nashville*, the first warship to display the
Confederate flag in the English Channel

Naval Historical Center

NAUTICAL TERMS

1. In naval terms, how does one refer to the right side of a ship?
2. What is the left side of a ship called?
3. What is the terminology for the front of a ship?
4. What is the rear of a ship called?
5. What frame member forms the backbone of a ship?
6. What is meant by the draft of a ship?
7. On Confederate cruisers the crew normally slept in what part of the ship?
8. What was the area called on board a warship where the officers lived?
9. What is the term for a number of men on board ship who eat or lodge together?
10. How does one refer to the center of a vessel?
11. What device can be used to keep a ship from drifting?
12. What stands upright in a sailing vessel and supports the sails and rigging?
13. What is a long piece of timber, tapering slightly toward the ends, and hung by the center to a mast to spread the square sails?
14. What is a yardarm?
15. What is the top of the mast called?
16. What is the most aft mast on a ship?
17. What is a holystone?
18. What is the normal term for the petty officer on a navy ship who attends the helm and binnacle at sea, and watches for signals, etc., while in port?
19. What is the box near the helm or wheel that contains the compass?
20. What is the name of the spar that extends the upper edges of a fore-and-aft sail?
21. What is the name of a pin, made of wood or iron, which is placed in a rail to hold gear secure?

NAUTICAL TERMS (ANSWERS)

1. Starboard side.
2. Port side.
3. The bow.
4. The stern.
5. The keel.
6. The depth of the ship in the water—the distance from the water line to the bottom of the keel.
7. The forecastle (pronounced *fōk's'l*) which was a raised deck near the bow.
8. The wardroom located in the stern of the ship.
9. Mess. The officers' mess or the enlisted men's mess.
10. Amidships.
11. An anchor.
12. The masts.
13. A yard.
14. The extremities of a yard.
15. The masthead.
16. The mizzenmast.
17. Soft sandstone, often used to scrub the decks of ships. Sailors knelt as if in prayer when scrubbing the decks. Also, holystone was often called so because it is full of holes.
18. The quartermaster.
19. The binnacle.
20. A gaff.
21. A belaying pin.

22. Semmes of the *Alabama* often describes himself as standing on the "horse block." What is a horse block?

23. Name the large spar projecting forward from a sailing vessel's bow.

24. On a Confederate ironclad, what was the name of the area occupied by the helmsman?

25. What is a funnel?

26. What is the area called where the sides of the hull and the flat bottom of a ship meet?

27. How does one refer to the widest portion of a ship?

28. What is another name for a propeller?

29. Many steam blockade runners used this type of propulsion.

30. What is meant by "standing watch"?

31. What is the name of the area where coal is stored on board?

32. Where was the ammunition stored on a warship?

33. What part of a steam engine converts the steam back to water?

34. These were used to lift the CSS *Tennessee* over the bar in Mobile Bay.

35. What do you call a square-rigged vessel with two masts?

36. What color were most blockade runners?

37. What was the common title given to a young boy who carried powder to the guns?

38. Why were some Union ironclads called double-enders?

39. Why were Confederate torpedo boats called "cigar boats"?

40. What was the terminology used for the exposed section of Confederate ironclads?

41. What is a kedge?

42. What was the designation given to the man who shoveled coal into the furnace?

43. What were range lights?

44. What is a warrant officer who has charge of the rigging, and summons the crew to duty called?

22. A raised platform at the very stern of the vessel where the commander can oversee all the activity on the ship.
23. The bowsprit.
24. The pilothouse.
25. A flue, or smokestack, which provides upward draft for the furnace and channels the escaping smoke above the vessel.
26. The bilge.
27. The widest part of any vessel is called its beam.
28. A screw.
29. Side-wheels.
30. An assigned length of time to be on duty, usually four hours.
31. The coal bunker.
32. In the magazine.
33. The condenser.
34. Camels. These were hollow vessels of iron or wood that, when filled with water, were sunk under the *Tennessee*. When the water was pumped out, the buoyancy of the camel raised the ironclad clear of the bar.
35. A brigantine.
36. Light gray or light blue which made them almost invisible on a dark night.
37. Powder monkey.
38. They had propellers at both ends and could steam in either direction.
39. From their shape.
40. The casemate. This armored housing surrounded the gun deck.
41. A small anchor.
42. A coal heaver.
43. A series of lights arranged in a row to guide blockade runners into a harbor.
44. The boatswain (pronounced *bō-s'n*).

45. Name the large timbers projecting from a vessel's side to which the anchor is raised and secured.

46. What was the chief instrument used by vessels at sea to determine their position?

47. A fathom is equal to how many feet?

48. In what unit of measurement is the speed of a ship determined?

49. What is the name of the area on board ship where meals are prepared?

50. On a warship, what is meant by "sounding general quarters"?

51. On a Confederate ironclad, what is the area called where the slanted armor of the casemate meets the deck?

52. What is meant by the term leeward?

45. Cathead.

46. The sextant.

47. A unit of measurement equal to six feet.

48. In knots, which is a division on a log line. One nautical mile equals 6,080 feet or 1.151 statute miles per hour.

49. The galley.

50. Each crewmember is to immediately report to his assigned battle station.

51. The knuckle.

52. The lee side. In a direction opposite to that from which the wind blows, which is called windward.

Nautical terms for the sails of a ship

1, Course; 1a, studding sails; 2, fore-topsail; 2a, studding sails; 3, main-topsail; 3a, studding sails; 4, mizzen-topsail; 5, fore-topgallant-sail; 5a, studding sails; 6, main-topgallant-sail; 6a, studding sails; 7, mizzen-topgallant-sail; 8, fore-royal-topsail; 8a, studding sails; 9, main-royal-topsail; 9a, studding sails; 10, mizzen-royal-topsail; 11, fore-skysail-topsail; 12, main-skysail-topsail; 13, mizzen-skysail-topsail; 14, fore-topmast staysail jib; 15, jib; 16, flying jib; 17, mizzen spanker; 18, spanker; 19, main-royal-staysail; 20, main-topmast-staysail; 21, mizzen-topgallant-staysail.

Internal view of the CSS *Shenandoah*

Author's Collection

THE BLOCKADE AND BLOCKADE RUNNERS

1. When was the blockade of the Southern coast proclaimed by Abraham Lincoln?
2. How many miles constituted the Confederate shoreline?
3. What were the three major Atlantic ports used by blockade runners along the Southern coast?
4. What were the three major Gulf ports used early in the war by blockade runners?
5. What major deep water anchorage was captured early in the war and served as a base for Union blockaders?
6. What two Southern states were included in Lincoln's extension of the blockade on April 27, 1861?
7. In the beginning, what was the ratio of blockade runners captured by the Union Navy?
8. What were the three most commonly used ports for blockade runners departing for the Confederacy?
9. What Mexican port was a favorite port of entry for blockade runners in the Gulf?
10. What huge Confederate fortification guarded the entrance to Wilmington, North Carolina?
11. What was the name of the Union naval unit charged with blockading the coasts of North Carolina and Virginia?
12. What nation's flag was flown by most blockade runners?
13. What percentage of the arms carried by Confederate armies was imported through the blockade?
14. Out of the estimated 1,300 attempts to run the blockade, how many were successful?
15. How many blockade runners were captured or destroyed by the Federal navy?
16. What blockade runner was named after a famous Southern general?
17. What percentage of blockade runners were owned by the Confederate government?
18. Who commanded these government-owned blockade runners?

THE BLOCKADE AND BLOCKADE RUNNERS (ANSWERS)

1. April 16, 1861.
2. Thirty-five hundred miles.
3. Wilmington, North Carolina; Charleston, South Carolina; and Savannah, Georgia.
4. Mobile, Alabama; New Orleans, Louisiana; and Galveston, Texas.
5. Port Royal, South Carolina. It was captured in early November of 1861.
6. Virginia and North Carolina.
7. One in nine.
8. Nassau, Bahamas; St. George, Bermuda; and Havana, Cuba.
9. Matamoros, Mexico.
10. Fort Fisher.
11. The North Atlantic Blockading Squadron.
12. Great Britain.
13. Roughly 60 percent.
14. Approximately one thousand.
15. Two hundred twenty-one.
16. The *Robert E. Lee.*
17. Approximately 25 percent.
18. Regular Confederate Navy officers.

19. How many blockade runners commanded by Confederate naval officers were captured?

20. What two brothers became famous as blockade runner captains?

21. What blockade runner was named in honor of the commander of Fort Fisher?

22. What South Carolina company became a major player in the blockade-running business?

23. Name two officers who began their Confederate Navy career commanding blockade runners.

24. When fired upon by a Union blockader, what Southern captain raised the Confederate flag and attempted to run down the enemy warship?

25. How many Union warships were eventually used in an attempt to enforce the blockade?

26. What Mexican port was frequently used by blockade runners?

27. How many successful runs through the blockade were made by the *Robert E. Lee*?

28. What did Lieutenant Usina always have with him as a good luck charm while commanding a blockade runner?

29. What was the name of a famous blockade runner purchased and operated by the state of North Carolina?

30. What ship was the war's most successful blockade runner?

31. How did the Confederacy pay for ships, arms, and munitions purchased abroad?

32. What was the name of the last steamer to clear a Confederate port?

33. What happened to many blockade runners after their capture?

34. When was the best time for a blockade runner to sail from a Southern port?

35. What persons were in great demand at Nassau, St. George's, and Havana?

36. Name one of two Florida ports that was a destination for some blockade runners.

37. What was the name of the last blockade runner commanded by John Newland Maffitt?

19. None.

20. Thomas and Robert Lockwood.

21. The *Colonel Lamb.*

22. The Fraser, Trenholm and Company.

23. Lieutenant John Newland Maffit and Lieutenant John Wilkinson.

24. Lieutenant Michael P. Usina. The Union ship turned and fled.

25. Approximately six hundred.

26. Matamoros. It was across the Rio Grande from Brownsville, Texas.

27. Fourteen.

28. His dog. The dog's name was Tinker.

29. The *Advance.*

30. The *Syren.* She made 33 trips through the blockade.

31. From the sale of cotton which was carried out by blockade runners.

32. The *Lark.* She arrived, unloaded, and escaped from Galveston on May 24, 1865.

33. Because of their great speed, blockade runners were taken into the Federal navy, armed, and added to the blockading fleet.

34. On a cloudy, moonless night.

35. Pilots who were familiar with the Southern coast.

36. St. Marks on the Gulf coast and New Smyrna on the Atlantic coast.

37. The *Owl.*

38. After safely making port at Wilmington on January 15, 1865, why did Maffitt turn his vessel around and speed out to sea?
39. Was the Federal blockade ever broken?
40. What kind of coal was used by blockade runners because it gave off such little smoke?
41. How did blockade runners vent their steam so it could not be heard?
42. Blockade runners built specifically for the trade were mostly constructed in these two countries.
43. What restrictions did the Confederate government impose on civilian blockade runners in March of 1864?
44. What famous Confederate spy drowned while trying to get to shore from the stranded blockade runner *Condor*?
45. How could some blockade runners make themselves less visible?
46. What is the estimated number of steamers that were ultimately utilized as blockade runners?

38. Fort Fisher had fallen to the Federals that same day.

39. Yes, for one day at Charleston on January 31, 1863, when two Confederate ironclads, the *Chicora* and the *Palmetto State*, attacked the blockading ships and drove them off.

40. Anthracite.

41. Under water.

42. England and Scotland.

43. Their inbound cargo had to be 50 percent military supplies.

44. Rose O'Neal Greenhow on October 1, 1864. She was buried with full military honors at Wilmington, North Carolina.

45. The vessels had hinged masts and smokestacks that could be lowered to the deck leaving only a few feet of the vessel visible above the water.

46. Three hundred.

The blockade runner *Robert E. Lee*

Naval Historical Center

The blockade runner *Colonel Lamb*

Naval Historical Center

Commander John Newland Maffitt

Naval Historical Center

Lieutenant Micheal P. Usina

Author's Collection

The blockade runner *Advance,* owned by the
state of North Carolina

Rose O'Neal Greenhow with her daughter, photographed
while in a Federal prison

**A blockade runner makes port under heavy fire
from the Union blockades**

The Navy Overseas

1. Who was the first Confederate naval officer assigned to Europe?
2. What was the primary mission of Confederate naval agents in Europe?
3. What famous oceanographer was assigned to Europe to, among other things, develop electric torpedoes?
4. What two cruisers did this officer procure for the Confederate Navy?
5. Name the French monarch who was sympathetic to the Southern cause.
6. What was the first Confederate warship to arrive in England?
7. At the beginning of the war, what did the Confederacy hope to accomplish by withholding shipments of cotton to Europe?
8. What proclamation did the British government issue on May 14, 1861?
9. What diplomatic status did the European powers extend to the Confederate States of America?
10. What British law prohibited English sailors from enlisting directly on Confederate ships?
11. What was the mission of Lieutenant James H. North when he was dispatched to Europe?
12. Name the first warship that Commander Bulloch contracted for.
13. Where was this ship built?
14. In what English shipyard was the CSS *Alabama* built?
15. What ship, destined for sale to the Confederacy, was seized by the British government and prompted a lengthy trial in English courts?
16. What French shipbuilder agreed to build four "clipper corvettes" for the Confederate Navy?
17. In the summer of 1863, how many Confederate warships were under construction in Europe?
18. Who became the ranking Confederate naval officer in Europe?

THE NAVY OVERSEAS (ANSWERS)

1. Commander James D. Bulloch.
2. To finance and procure ships, and get them to sea fully armed, manned, and equipped.
3. Matthew Fountain Maury. He left Charleston, South Carolina, on October 9, 1862.
4. The CSS *Georgia* and the CSS *Rappahannock*. The *Rappahannock* never got to sea and was used as a receiving ship.
5. Emperor Napoleon III.
6. The CSS *Nashville*. She arrived in Southampton on November 21, 1861.
7. They hoped to create a shortage of cotton which would force France and England to intervene in the war.
8. A Proclamation of Neutrality.
9. The status of "belligerents." This status guaranteed recognition of the Confederacy by all neutrals as a legitimate war-making state, and accorded Confederate ships' treatment as regularly commissioned naval vessels.
10. The Foreign Enlistment Act of 1819.
11. North was to purchase or build ironclad vessels that could break the blockade.
12. The CSS *Florida*.
13. At the William C. Miller & Sons Shipyard, Liverpool, England.
14. John Laird & Sons of Birkenhead across the Mersey River from Liverpool, England.
15. The *Alexandra*.
16. Lucien Armam.
17. Ten—four ironclad rams, one larger ironclad, and five composite cruisers.
18. Captain Samuel Barron, Sr.

19. In addition to the *Alabama* and *Florida*, what other famous cruiser did Bulloch manage to get to sea?

20. The sale of cotton bonds at the exchanges in London, Paris, Frankfort, Amsterdam, and Liverpool financed what loan?

21. Of the numerous ironclads designed and constructed for the Confederacy in Europe, which was the only one delivered?

22. What were the names of the two Confederate ironclads built by the Laird Shipyard in Birkenhead?

23. What naval event almost precipitated war between the United States and England?

24. What was the most formidable feature of the two ironclads constructed at the Laird Shipyard?

25. Who was the Confederate government's minister to Great Britain?

26. Who was the Confederacy's minister to France?

27. Name the British prime minister during the war.

28. What was the name given to the ironclad built at the Thomson Shipyard on the Clyde River in Glasgow, Scotland?

29. Who commanded the ironclad CSS *Stonewall* when she left France?

30. Where did Commander Bulloch settle after the war?

19. The CSS *Shenandoah*.

20. The Erlanger Loan.

21. The CSS *Stonewall*. She arrived in Havana, Cuba, after the war had ended.

22. The CSS *North Carolina* and the CSS *Mississippi*.

23. The "Trent Affair." The British mail steamer *Trent* was stopped on the high seas by the USS *San Jacinto*, and Confederate diplomats James Mason and John Slidell were removed at gunpoint.

24. Forward and aft turret, each with two very heavy guns.

25. James Mason.

26. John Slidell.

27. Lord Henry J. T. Palmerston.

28. *Number 61*. Later historians dubbed her the Scottish Sea Monster.

29. Captain Thomas J. Page.

30. Liverpool, England. Bulloch never returned to the South.

Commander James D.
Bulloch, Confederate
naval agent in Europe

Naval Historical Center

Commander Matthew
Fontaine Maury

Library of Congress

The CSS *Alexandra* was seized by British authorities and never reached the Confederacy

Naval Historical Center

Captain Samuel Barron, Sr.

The flag officer commanding Confederate naval forces in Europe.

Author's Collection

The HMS *Wivern,* the intended CSS *North Carolina,*
photographed in 1865

Contemporary view of the Laird Shipyard at Birkenhead,
England, where the CSS *Alabama* was built

Number 61, the Scottish Sea Monster, being fitted out on the
Clyde River in Scotland

London Illustrated News

The CSS *Stonewall*, the only European-built armored warship to
actually be delivered to the Confederate Navy

Naval Historical Center

IRONCLADS AND GUNBOATS

1. Name the first Confederate ironclad to be taken into battle.
2. Who commanded the Confederacy's first ironclad?
3. How many guns were mounted on the CSS *Manassas*?
4. What was the principal weapon of the *Manassas*?
5. In addition to the ironclad *Manassas*, name two of the Confederate gunboats that took part in the battle of October 12, 1861, at the Head of the Passes.
6. Name the Confederate commander of the *McRae* who was mortally wounded at the Battle of New Orleans, April 24, 1862.
7. What Confederate ironclad had two center paddle wheels, fore and aft, and two propellers at the stern?
8. How many guns were eventually mounted on the *Louisiana*?
9. Who commanded the unfinished *Louisiana* at the Battle of New Orleans?
10. What other large ironclad was nearing completion at the time of Admiral Farragut's attack on New Orleans?
11. What two brothers designed and built the CSS *Mississippi*?
12. Who was the executive officer of the *McRae* who took command when Lieutenant Huger was wounded at the Battle of New Orleans?
13. What gunboat of the Louisiana state navy put up a terrific fight at the Battle of New Orleans?
14. What constituted the *Louisiana*'s casemate armor?
15. How was the *Louisiana* utilized at the Battle of New Orleans?
16. What was the ultimate fate of the *Louisiana*?
17. What Confederate officer, who would later command a cruiser at sea, ordered the destruction of the CSS *Mississippi*?
18. At the time of the fall of New Orleans, what two ironclads were being constructed at Memphis, Tennessee?
19. The gunboat *McRae*, before her loss at New Orleans, fought to save what island fortification?

IRONCLADS AND GUNBOATS (ANSWERS)

1. The CSS *Manassas*. She attacked the Federals at the Head of the Passes below New Orleans on October 12, 1861.

2. First Lieutenant Alexander F. Warley.

3. One—an old 9-inch Dahlgren smoothbore protruded from the bow. It was difficult to load and impossible to aim.

4. Its cast iron ram.

5. The CSS *McRae*, the CSS *Tuscarora*, and the CSS *Ivy*.

6. First Lieutenant Thomas B. Huger.

7. The CSS *Louisiana*. The installation of the two propellers was never completed.

8. Sixteen.

9. Commander Charles F. McIntosh. He was mortally wounded during the battle and died on May 17, 1862.

10. The CSS *Mississippi*. The huge unfinished ironclad that weighed over four thousand tons and intended to carry 20 heavy guns had to be destroyed to keep her from falling into the hands of the enemy.

11. The Tifts—Nelson and Asa.

12. Lieutenant Charles W. Read.

13. The LSN *Governor Moore*.

14. Interlocking railroad rails mounted on a 45-degree slant.

15. As a floating battery. With her propellers still not connected, she could not move.

16. She was destroyed by her own crew.

17. Lieutenant James I. Waddell.

18. The CSS *Arkansas* and the CSS *Tennessee*. The *Tennessee* is not to be confused with the warship of the same name that fought two years later at the Battle of Mobile Bay.

19. Island No. 10 on the upper Mississippi River.

20. Of the nine Confederate gunboats involved in the Battle of Memphis on June 6, 1862, what was the name of the only one to survive?

21. What was the fate of the *Arkansas* and *Tennessee* upon the fall of Memphis?

22. Where was the *Arkansas*'s construction completed?

23. What was unique about the *Arkansas*'s casemate?

24. Name the steamer that acted as living quarters for the workers laboring on the *Arkansas*.

25. Who became commander of the *Arkansas*?

26. Where were the engines for the *Arkansas* built?

27. What were the *Arkansas*'s length, beam, and draft?

28. How many guns did the *Arkansas* carry?

29. After the *Arkansas* was completed, what Confederate officer ordered her to come to Vicksburg?

30. When did the *Arkansas* leave Yazoo City for her run to Vicksburg?

31. What three enemy vessels did the *Arkansas* encounter in the Yazoo River?

32. Which of these three enemy vessels was severely damaged and driven ashore by the *Arkansas*?

33. Upon entering the Mississippi, what stood between the *Arkansas* and the safe haven of Vicksburg?

34. Who was the pilot who stood at the wheel of the *Arkansas* as she steamed through the two Federal fleets?

35. When the *Arkansas* finally reached Vicksburg, what was the number of casualties on board?

36. What two Federal vessels attacked the *Arkansas* on July 22, 1862, while moored at Vicksburg?

37. Why was the *Arkansas* sent south down river by Major General Earl Van Dorn?

38. What happened to the *Arkansas* at Baton Rouge?

39. Who was in command of the *Arkansas* at the time of her destruction?

40. What Federal vessel claimed credit for destroying the *Arkansas*?

20. The CSS *General Earl Van Dorn.*

21. The unfinished *Arkansas* was towed down the Mississippi River and into the Yazoo River; the uncompleted *Tennessee* had to be destroyed.

22. Yazoo City, Mississippi.

23. The armored sides were vertical unlike other Confederate ironclads.

24. The *Capitol.*

25. Commander Isaac N. Brown, who was from Kentucky, but at the time of the war he was a resident of Mississippi.

26. Memphis, Tennessee.

27. One hundred sixty-five feet in length, 35 feet abeam, and 14 feet draft.

28. Ten—two 8-inch Columbiads, two 9-inch Dahlgrens, two 32-pounders, and four 6-inch rifles.

29. Major General Earl Van Dorn.

30. July 12, 1862.

31. The ironclad USS *Carondelet*, the "timberclad" USS *Tyler*, and the army ram USS *Queen of the West.*

32. The USS *Carondelet.*

33. The combined fleets of Admiral Farragut and Commodore Davis, a force of more than 30 warships.

34. Pilot James Brady.

35. Twenty-five. Ten killed and 15 wounded.

36. The ironclad USS *Essex* and the army ram USS *Queen of the West.*

37. To aid in the attempted recapture of Baton Rouge, Louisiana.

38. She was destroyed by her own crew when her machinery became inoperative.

39. Lieutenant Henry K. Stevens. He was the executive officer.

40. The USS *Essex.*

41. What U.S. warship provided the lower hull and engines for the ironclad CSS *Virginia*?

42. What two Confederate officers were responsible for the design of the *Virginia*?

43. Where did the construction of the *Virginia* take place?

44. The *Merrimack* had been burned and scuttled. Who was responsible for refurbishing her engines?

45. What did the *Virginia*'s casemate have that no other Confederate ironclad had?

46. Where were the iron plates rolled for the *Virginia*'s casemate?

47. What Confederate officer determined the best slant angle for an armored casemate?

48. What was this slant angle?

49. What particularly devastating guns were carried by the *Virginia*?

50. What was the thickness of the iron plating on the *Virginia*?

51. When was the *Virginia* launched?

52. What was the length and weight of the *Virginia*?

53. What was the *Virginia*'s maximum speed?

54. Who did Secretary Mallory appoint as the *Virginia*'s commander?

55. Name the executive officer of the *Virginia*.

56. What was unique about the *Virginia*'s bow and stern?

57. What was the weight of the *Virginia*'s ram?

58. How did the *Virginia* sink the USS *Cumberland*?

59. How did the *Virginia* destroy the USS *Congress*?

60. What distinct advantage did the USS *Monitor* have over the *Virginia*?

61. Name the other Confederate warships that participated in the two-day Battle of Hampton Roads.

62. The little *Teaser* would become famous for what event?

63. What would the *Patrick Henry* become noted for later in the war?

64. Who commanded the *Virginia* during her fight with the *Monitor*?

41. The USS *Merrimack*.
42. Commander John M. Brooke and Chief Constructor John L. Porter.
43. In dry dock No. 1 at the Gosport Naval Shipyard, Portsmouth, Virginia.
44. Chief Engineer William P. Williamson.
45. Rounded ends.
46. At the Tredegar Iron Works, Richmond, Virginia.
47. John M. Brooke.
48. Thirty-six degrees.
49. Six 9-inch Dahlgren smoothbores, two 6.4-inch Brooke rifles, and two 7-inch Brooke rifles in fore-and-aft pivots.
50. Four inches. Two layers of 2-inch plates.
51. February 17, 1862.
52. Two hundred sixty-three feet and thirty-two hundred tons.
53. Approximately nine knots.
54. Captain (later Admiral) Franklin Buchanan. Actually, Buchanan was commander of the James River Squadron and flew his flag from the *Virginia*.
55. Lieutenant Catesby ap R. Jones.
56. They were both submerged.
57. Fifteen hundred pounds.
58. By ramming her.
59. By gunfire.
60. The *Monitor* was faster and more maneuverable.
61. The CSS *Raleigh*, the CSS *Beaufort*, the CSS *Teaser*, the CSS *Jamestown*, and the CSS *Patrick Henry*.
62. She became the world's first "aircraft carrier" when Confederates launched an observation balloon from her deck during the Peninsula campaign.
63. The *Patrick Henry* became the Confederate Naval Academy's school ship.
64. Lieutenant Catesby ap R. Jones. Buchanan had been wounded the previous day.

65. How many casualties were sustained on the *Virginia*?
66. Who replaced the wounded Buchanan as the *Virginia*'s new commander?
67. Why did it become necessary to destroy the *Virginia*?
68. When was the *Virginia* destroyed?
69. What unfinished ironclad was saved when Norfolk was abandoned?
70. Has any part of the *Virginia* survived to this day?
71. What Confederate gunboat was sunk as an obstruction at Drewry's Bluff in the James River?
72. What famous Confederate ironclad was built at Selma, Alabama?
73. Who was the builder of the CSS *Tennessee*?
74. What rolling mill fabricated the iron plates for the *Tennessee*?
75. Who was selected to be the *Tennessee*'s captain?
76. Who was the designer of the *Tennessee*?
77. From where did the *Tennessee*'s builders obtain her engines?
78. When was the *Tennessee* launched?
79. What two steamers towed the unfinished *Tennessee* 160 miles down the Alabama River to the city of Mobile?
80. What was the thickness of the *Tennessee*'s armor?
81. What constituted the *Tennessee*'s armament?
82. What would prove to be the *Tennessee*'s greatest flaw?
83. What device was used to raise the *Tennessee* and allow her to clear the bar into the lower part of Mobile Bay?
84. Name the Confederate admiral, commander of the Mobile Squadron, who flew his flag from the *Tennessee*?
85. In addition to the *Tennessee*, what three gunboats comprised the Mobile Squadron?
86. What two additional ironclads, built by Henry D. Bassett and having weak engines, were utilized as floating batteries at Mobile?
87. When Farragut's attack came at Mobile on August 5, 1864, how many men comprised the *Tennessee*'s crew?

65. Ten—two killed and eight wounded.

66. Captain Josiah Tattnall.

67. Upon the Confederate evacuation of Norfolk, it was discovered that her draft was too great to enable her to pass up the James River.

68. May 11, 1862.

69. The *Richmond* was towed up the James River by the CSS *Patrick Henry*. She was completed at Richmond.

70. Yes. An anchor and part of her propeller shaft are on display at the Museum of the Confederacy in Richmond. A few pieces of her armor plate are in the Portsmouth Naval Shipyard Museum in Portsmouth, Virginia.

71. The *Jamestown*.

72. The CSS *Tennessee*.

73. Henry D. Bassett.

74. The armor for the *Tennessee* was rolled by the Schofield and Markham Iron Works, in Atlanta, Georgia.

75. Commander James D. Johnston.

76. Chief Constructor John L. Porter designed a majority of the ironclads produced by the Confederacy.

77. From the side-wheel steamer *Alonzo Child*.

78. February 8, 1863.

79. The *Baltic* and the *Southern Republic*.

80. Six inches to just aft of the pilothouse, the remainder being five inches.

81. Two 7-inch Brooke rifles mounted on pivots fore and aft, and four 6.4-inch Brooke rifles in broadside.

82. Her exposed rudder chains which were easily damaged by enemy fire.

83. Camels. Large tanks filled with water were strapped to her sides, and when the water was pumped out, it raised the vessel high enough to clear the bar.

84. Admiral Franklin Buchanan, who had recovered from his wound suffered at the Battle of Hampton Roads.

85. The CSS *Selma*, the CSS *Morgan*, and the CSS *Gaines*.

86. The CSS *Tuscaloosa* and the CSS *Huntsville*.

87. Eighteen officers and 143 men.

88. What was the fate of the three Confederate gunboats at the Battle of Mobile Bay?

89. What was the fate of the *Tennessee* in the Battle of Mobile Bay?

90. What was the final disposition of the *Tennessee*?

91. What two Confederate ironclads temporarily broke the blockade at Charleston, South Carolina?

92. What ironclad had three "regularly enlisted" free Negroes as part of her crew?

93. Who contributed the monies for the construction of the *Palmetto State*?

94. Who was the builder of the *Palmetto State*?

95. What was unique about the *Palmetto State*'s pilothouse?

96. What was the first ironclad to be launched at Charleston?

97. Where did the engines for the *Palmetto State* come from?

98. What was the *Chicora*'s most glaring deficiency?

99. On what former ironclad had many of the crew of the *Chicora* and *Palmetto State* served?

100. Who were the commanders of the *Chicora* and *Palmetto State* when they attacked the Federal blockaders on January 30, 1863?

101. What new Confederate ironclad joined the Charleston Squadron late in the war?

102. Who was this ironclad's commander?

103. What was the fate of the ironclads attached to the Charleston Squadron?

104. Name the ironclad that was nearing completion on the Chattahoochee River at Columbus, Georgia, when the war ended.

105. What was the name of the Confederate gunboat whose boiler explosion killed 18 men on May 27, 1863?

106. What two cotton-protected gunboats were instrumental in the recapture of Galveston, Texas?

107. What Louisiana gunboat fought the advancing enemy while backing up a narrow bayou?

88. The *Gaines* and the *Selma* were destroyed; the *Morgan* escaped to Mobile.

89. After being surrounded and subjected to a terrific pounding by Federal warships, she was forced to surrender.

90. She was commissioned into the Union Navy as the USS *Tennessee*.

91. The CSS *Chicora* and the CSS *Palmetto State* attacked and drove off the Federal blockading ships on January 30, 1863.

92. The *Chicora*.

93. The women of Charleston had donated the money.

94. Cameron and Company of Charleston.

95. The pilothouse was to the rear of the smokestack.

96. The *Chicora* on August 23, 1862.

97. From the gunboat CSS *Lady Davis*.

98. With only one engine she could barely make five knots.

99. The CSS *Arkansas*.

100. Captain John R. Tucker commanded the *Chicora*, and First Lieutenant John Rutledge commanded the *Palmetto State*.

101. The CSS *Charleston* joined the squadron in early 1864.

102. Commander Isaac N. Brown.

103. All were destroyed by their crews when Charleston was evacuated on February 18, 1865.

104. The CSS *Jackson*.

105. The CSS *Chattahoochee*.

106. The CSS *Bayou City* and the CSS *Neptune*.

107. The CSS *J. A. Cotton*.

108. Who was the commander of this gunboat?
109. What ironclad was known as the "ironclad built in a cornfield"?
110. Where was the actual construction site of the CSS *Albemarle*?
111. Name the builder of the *Albemarle*.
112. What was the armament of the *Albemarle*?
113. Upon launching on October 6, 1863, the *Albemarle* was towed upriver to what North Carolina town?
114. Who was selected by the Navy Department to command the *Albemarle*?
115. When was the *Albemarle* commissioned?
116. Where and when did the *Albemarle* first engage the enemy?
117. What Union warship did the *Albemarle* sink in her first engagement?
118. What two gunboats accompanied the *Albemarle* on May 5, 1864, when she steamed into Albemarle Sound?
119. Name the executive officer of the *Albemarle*.
120. What courageous Union officer succeeded in sinking the *Albemarle*?
121. Who was commander of the *Albemarle* at the time of her sinking?
122. What was the name of the sister ship to the *Albemarle*?
123. Where was the *Albemarle*'s sister ironclad built?
124. Who was the builder of the CSS *Neuse*?
125. What was the eventual fate of the *Neuse*?
126. What Confederate ironclad attacked the Federal blockaders off the mouth of the Cape Fear River?
127. Where was the CSS *Raleigh* constructed?
128. Who was the commander of the *Raleigh* when she attacked the Federal blockaders?
129. Name the two Confederate gunboats that accompanied the *Raleigh* in the attack on the Union blockaders.
130. Why was the *Raleigh* never used again after this sortie?
131. What other ironclad was built at Wilmington, North Carolina?

108. Ed Fuller. He was a civilian steamboat captain, and although wounded in both arms, managed to steer the *Cotton* with his feet.

109. The CSS *Albemarle.*

110. The *Albemarle* was built at Edwards Ferry on the Roanoke River, North Carolina.

111. Army Lieutenant Gilbert Elliott.

112. Two Brooke 6.4-inch rifles mounted on pivots fore and aft.

113. The *Albemarle* was towed to Halifax, North Carolina, to have her armor, engines, and machinery installed.

114. Commander James W. Cooke, a native of North Carolina.

115. April 17, 1864.

116. At Plymouth, North Carolina, April 18, 1864.

117. The USS *Southfield.*

118. The CSS *Bombshell* and the CSS *Cotton Plant.*

119. First Lieutenant Francis M. Roby.

120. Lieutenant William B. Cushing.

121. First Lieutenant Alexander P. Warley.

122. The CSS *Neuse.*

123. The *Neuse* was built at White Hall on the banks of the Neuse River, North Carolina.

124. Howard & Ellis Shipbuilders.

125. After shelling the approaching Union cavalry, she was set on fire by her own crew on March 12, 1865. Her unburned hull was recovered in the 1960s, and is now on display at the Caswell/Neuse State Historic Site near Kinston, North Carolina.

126. The CSS *Raleigh.*

127. Wilmington, North Carolina. The *Raleigh* was constructed in the shipyard of J. L. Cassidy & Sons, located at the foot of Church Street.

128. First Lieutenant J. Pembroke Jones.

129. The CSS *Yadkin* and the CSS *Equator.*

130. She ran aground on her return and "broke her back" (her keel snapped). Her armor and guns were salvaged.

131. The CSS *North Carolina.*

132. Who was the commander of the CSS *North Carolina*?

133. What would be the *North Carolina*'s ultimate fate?

134. Name the ironclad that was constructed from a former blockade runner.

135. Where was this ironclad built?

136. Who were the builders of the CSS *Atlanta*?

137. When was the *Atlanta* commissioned?

138. What was the *Atlanta*'s maximum speed?

139. How many guns did the *Atlanta* carry?

140. Who commanded the *Atlanta* at the time of her capture?

141. What was the fate of the *Atlanta*?

142. What three ironclads formed part of the James River Squadron?

143. What two small gunboats that fought in the early days of the conflict were still operational and attached to the James River Squadron at the end of the war?

144. How many guns did the *Richmond* carry?

145. What was the maximum speed of the *Richmond*?

146. When was the *Fredericksburg* commissioned?

147. What was unique about the *Fredericksburg*'s casemate?

148. Who was the first commander of the *Virginia II*?

149. How thick was the armor on the *Virginia II*?

150. Which two ironclads of the James River Squadron took a pounding from Federal guns at the Battle of Trent's Reach?

151. What speedy Confederate gunboat attempted to run the blockade of the Mississippi River long after Lee's troops had surrendered at Appomattox?

152. What powerful Union side-wheel steamer was captured and commissioned into the Confederate Navy?

153. What Confederate ironclad was still on the stocks at Richmond and had to be destroyed when the city was evacuated?

154. Name the Confederate ironclad built at Shreveport, Louisiana.

155. What was unique about the *Missouri*'s propulsion system?

132. Commander William T. Muse.

133. Her hull became so worm-eaten that she sank at her moorings on September 27, 1864.

134. The CSS *Atlanta* was constructed from the former blockade runner *Fingal*.

135. Savannah, Georgia.

136. The Tifts—brothers Asa and Nelson.

137. November 22, 1863.

138. Ten knots.

139. Four—two 7-inch Brooke rifles and two 6.4-inch Brooke rifles.

140. Commander William A. Webb.

141. After running aground in Wassaw Sound near Savannah, she was captured by the USS *Weehawken* on June 17, 1863, and taken into the U.S. Navy as the USS *Atlanta*. She served with the Federals on the James River until the end of the war.

142. The CSS *Richmond*, the CSS *Fredericksburg*, and the CSS *Virginia II*.

143. The CSS *Beaufort* and the CSS *Raleigh*.

144. The *Richmond* carried four 7-inch Brooke rifles.

145. Five to six knots.

146. The *Fredericksburg* was commissioned in March of 1863.

147. She had a pilothouse at both ends.

148. Commander Robert B. Pegram.

149. Six inches forward and five inches aft.

150. The *Richmond* and the *Virginia II*.

151. The CSS *William H. Webb*.

152. The CSS *Water Witch*. She was captured from the Federals in Ossabaw Sound, Georgia, on June 3, 1864.

153. The CSS *Texas*.

154. The CSS *Missouri*.

155. The *Missouri* was driven by an immense center paddle wheel.

156. What ironclad was surrendered to the Federals at Nanna Hubba, Alabama, on May 10, 1865?

157. What two ironclads had engines so weak that they were utilized as floating batteries at Savannah and New Orleans?

158. What ironclad was the flagship of the Savannah Squadron?

159. What gunboat operated as the flagship of Confederate naval forces at Wilmington, North Carolina?

160. What was the name of the last Confederate ironclad to surrender to United States forces at the end of the war?

156. The CSS *Nashville.*

157. The CSS *Georgia* at Savannah and the CSS *New Orleans* at New Orleans.

158. The CSS *Savannah*, considered one of the best ironclads produced by the Confederacy.

159. The CSS *Yadkin.*

160. The CSS *Missouri* surrendered at Shreveport, Louisiana, on June 3, 1865.

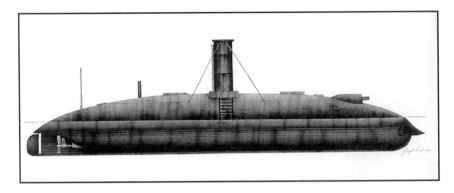

The CSS *Manassas*

The CSS *McRae*

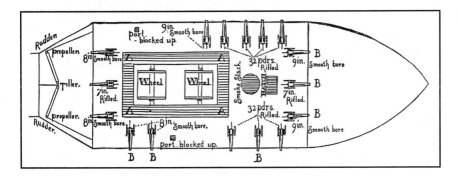

The gun deck of the CSS *Louisiana*, from a sketch made by Commander John K. Mitchell

Official Records Navy

The CSS *Arkansas*

Naval Historical Center

The CSS *Virginia*

Naval Historical Center

The CSS *Richmond*

Naval Historical Center

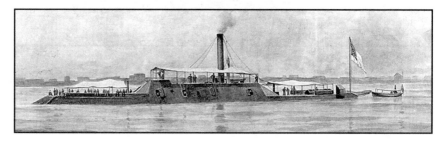

The CSS *Tennessee*

Naval Historical Center

The CSS *Palmetto State*

The CSS *Albemarle*

The CSS *Atlanta*

TORPEDO WARFARE

1. What Union warship was the first to encounter Confederate torpedoes?

2. What Confederate officer is known as the Father of Mine Warfare?

3. With what type of mine, or torpedo as it was termed then, did the Father of Mine Warfare experiment?

4. Who took over the Submarine Battery Service when Commander Maury was transferred to Europe?

5. What were two of the most common types of defensive torpedoes devised?

6. Name the Confederate officer who is credited with inventing these two types of torpedoes.

7. What Union ironclad became the first Federal warship to be sunk by a Confederate torpedo?

8. Name the Confederate submarine that was built as a privateer.

9. Where was this privateer submarine built?

10. Who were the designers and fabricators of this submarine?

11. Who was the chief financier of the submarine *Pioneer*?

12. What young Confederate Army officer developed a chemical fuse for detonating torpedoes?

13. What type of torpedo was responsible for sinking the USS *Cairo*?

14. Who is generally acknowledged as the inventor of the spar torpedo?

15. What type of vessel did Captain Lee utilize in his first experiment with a spar torpedo?

16. What was the Special Service Detachment which operated at Charleston?

17. What Union monitor was sunk by a Confederate torpedo at the Battle of Mobile Bay?

18. Name the first Confederate vessel designed specifically as a torpedo boat.

19. Where was this first torpedo boat constructed?

TORPEDO WARFARE (ANSWERS)

1. The USS *Pawnee* encountered floating torpedoes in the Potomac River on July 7, 1861.
2. Commander Matthew Fontaine Maury.
3. Floating torpedoes electrically detonated.
4. Lieutenant Hunter Davidson.
5. The keg torpedo, constructed from a wooden barrel, and the frame torpedo which incorporated torpedoes fixed to a wooden frame and sunk in a main shipping channel.
6. Brigadier General Gabriel J. Rains.
7. The USS *Cairo* was sunk in the Yazoo River, Mississippi, on December 13, 1862.
8. The *Pioneer*.
9. New Orleans, Louisiana.
10. James McClintock and Baxter Watson.
11. Horace L. Hunley.
12. Captain Francis D. Lee.
13. A glass demijohn which was detonated by a friction primer connected to a lanyard.
14. Captain Francis D. Lee.
15. A canoe.
16. A contingent of sailors manning rowboats equipped with spar torpedoes.
17. The USS *Tecumseh* went down on August 5, 1864, with the loss of 93 men.
18. The CSS *Torch*.
19. Charleston, South Carolina.

20. Who was the designer of the CSS *Torch*?

21. Name the two men who designed what many considered to be the best floating torpedo of the war.

22. What type of torpedo destroyed the USS *Commodore Jones* in the James River on June 6, 1864?

23. What class of Confederate torpedo boats was often referred to as "cigar boats"?

24. What was the commissioned name of the first David class torpedo boat to be completed?

25. Who was the builder of this first David class torpedo boat?

26. Who commanded the CSS *David* on her first attack on a Union warship?

27. What Union warship was attacked by the *David* off Charleston, South Carolina?

28. Who was the engineer who brought the *David* safely back into port after the attack on the *New Ironsides*?

29. What was the name of the second submarine built by James McClintock and Baxter Watson?

30. What happened to this submarine?

31. What was the name of the third and final submarine built by McClintock and Watson?

32. How was the CSS *H. L. Hunley* transported to Charleston, South Carolina?

33. How many times did the *Hunley* sink?

34. Who was piloting the *Hunley* when it failed to surface on October 15, 1863?

35. What Union vessel was the *Hunley* finally successful in sinking?

36. Who commanded the *Hunley* on this historic mission?

37. Besides the David class, what other class of torpedo boats were constructed by the Confederacy?

38. What was the commissioned name of the first Squib class torpedo boat?

39. Who commanded this first Squib class boat?

40. What Federal warship was attacked by the CSS *Squib*?

20. Captain Francis D. Lee.

21. E. C. Singer and Dr. J. R. Fretwell.

22. A tank torpedo containing two thousand pounds of powder which was electrically detonated by a man on shore.

23. David class.

24. The CSS *David*.

25. David C. Ebaugh, a machinist working for Dr. St. Julien Ravenal and Theodore Stoney of Charleston, South Carolina.

26. Lieutenant William T. Glassell.

27. The USS *New Ironsides* was severely damaged by the *David*'s torpedo on October 5, 1863.

28. Chief Engineer James H. Tomb.

29. *American Diver* (also known as *Pioneer II*).

30. The *American Diver* sank in rough seas at the entrance to Mobile Bay in early February 1863.

31. The *H. L. Hunley*, which was launched at Mobile in mid-July 1863.

32. By railroad flatcar.

33. Three times—twice by accident and the third time on her last operational sortie.

34. Horace L. Hunley.

35. The USS *Housatonic*, on February 17, 1864.

36. Lieutenant George E. Dixon, CSA.

37. Squib class.

38. The CSS *Squib*.

39. Lieutenant Hunter Davidson.

40. The USS *Minnesota* in Hampton Roads, Virginia, on April 8, 1864.

41. What type of torpedo caused the huge explosion at the Union supply depot at City Point, Virginia?
42. Name the Squib class torpedo boat that was built at Columbus, Georgia.
43. What three Squib class torpedo boats were part of the James River Squadron?
44. Name the David class torpedo boat that was put on display at the Brooklyn Navy Yard after the war.
45. Where was the submarine built that was tested in the James River?
46. Name the torpedo boat that attacked the USS *Octorara* in Mobile Bay on January 27, 1865.
47. During the war, how many Union vessels were sunk by Confederate torpedoes?
48. What was the last Union vessel of the war to be destroyed by a Confederate torpedo?

41. A clock-work torpedo disguised in a wooden case labeled "candles."

42. The CSS *Viper*.

43. The CSS *Hornet*, the CSS *Wasp*, and the CSS *Scorpion*.

44. The CSS *Midge*.

45. The Tredegar Iron Works, Richmond, Virginia.

46. The CSS *St. Patrick*.

47. Twenty-nine. Fourteen additional vessels received from minor to serious damage.

48. The USS *R. B. Hamilton*. The army transport struck a torpedo and sank in Mobile Bay on May 12, 1865.

Lieutenant Hunter Davidson

Naval Historical Center

James R. McClintock

Naval Historical Center

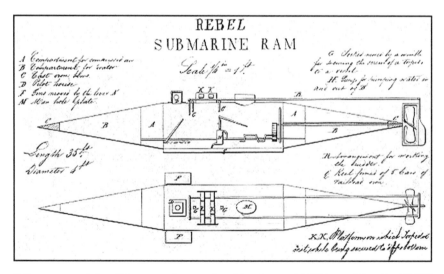

Diagram of the *Pioneer* drawn by Engineer William Shock, USN

Naval Historical Center

Horace L. Hunley

Naval Historical Center

Chief Engineer
James H. Tomb

Southern Historical Collection,
Wilson Library, UNC

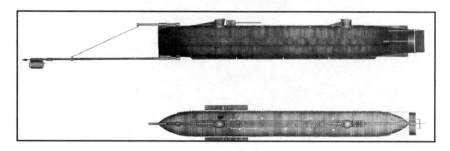

The CSS *H. L. Hunley*

Joseph Hinds, Illustrator

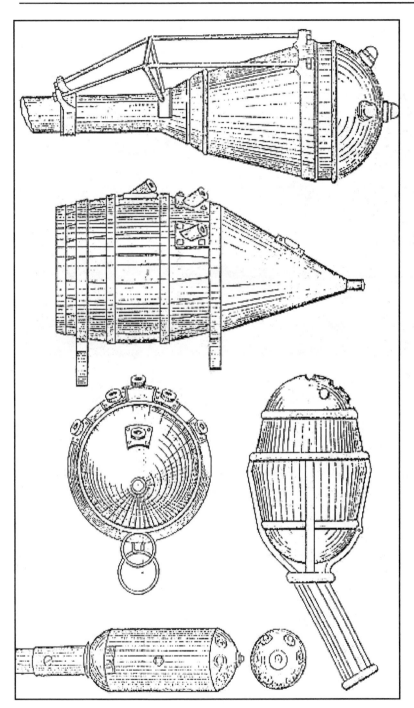

Several types of spar torpedoes used by the Confederate Navy

Official Records Navy

The CSS *Midge* on display at the Brooklyn Navy Yard after the war

Naval Historical Center

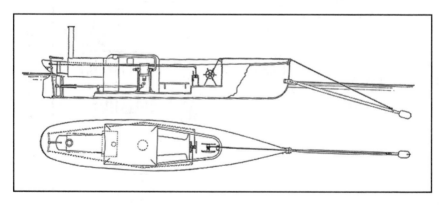

Drawing of the CSS *Squib*

Official Records Navy

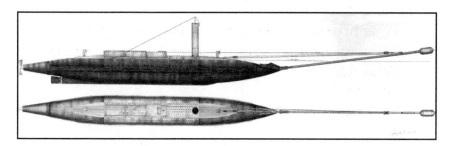

The CSS *David*

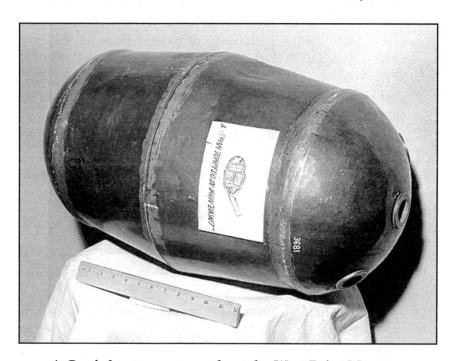

A Confederate spar torpedo at the West Point Museum

Naval Ordnance

1. What was the most sought after naval gun manufactured in the Confederacy?

2. What two sizes of this gun were the most popular?

3. What was the navy's equivalent of the infantry sword?

4. What enabled a heavy gun to be aimed and fired in different directions?

5. How many men comprised a typical gun crew on a heavy pivot rifle?

6. Name two facilities in the Confederacy that produced heavy guns for the navy.

7. What revolver was imported from England and carried by many Confederate naval officers?

8. How many heavy guns were recovered from the Gosport Navy Shipyard at Portsmouth after its abandonment by the Federals?

9. What bureau at the Navy Department in Richmond was responsible for naval ordnance?

10. How was the size of guns designed to fire explosive shells usually stated?

11. How was the size of guns designed to fire solid shot usually stated?

12. What was the total weight, minus the carriage, of a 7-inch Brooke rifle?

13. How were the reinforcing bands on a Brooke rifle applied?

14. How many Brooke rifles were produced by the Naval Gun Foundry at Selma?

15. Name the English pivot guns mounted on the cruiser CSS *Florida*.

16. Who was the manufacturer of the forward pivot gun on the *Alabama*?

17. Where was the Confederate Naval Gun Foundry located?

18. Who was superintendent of the Confederate Naval Gun Foundry?

NAVAL ORDNANCE (ANSWERS)

1. The Brooke rifle designed by Commander John M. Brooke.
2. 6.4-inch and 7-inch.
3. The cutlass.
4. The pivot mount.
5. Twenty-seven.
6. Tredegar Iron Works in Richmond, Virginia, and the Naval Gun Foundry at Selma, Alabama.
7. The Kerr .44-caliber, five chambered revolver.
8. One thousand one hundred ninety-eight.
9. The Office of Ordnance and Hydrography.
10. The diameter of the bore in inches.
11. The weight of their solid shot.
12. Fifteen thousand pounds.
13. Shrink-on method.
14. Fifty-five. Fifteen 6.4-inch, thirty-nine 7-inch, and one 11-inch. One hundred two Brookes were in various stages of production at the end of the war.
15. Blakely 7-inch rifles.
16. Blakely. The 7-inch 110-pounder pivot rifle was raised from the ocean floor in 1995 and found to be loaded. The black powder was still dry.
17. Selma, Alabama.
18. Commander Catesby ap R. Jones.

19. What naval officer conducted test firings of the *Virginia's* guns prior to their being placed on board?

20. What was the armament of the most heavily armed Confederate ironclad, the *Virginia II*?

21. What was the weight of the 6.4-inch Brooke rifle?

22. Where were the Brooke rifles on the CSS *Atlanta* manufactured?

23. What North Carolina facility was the sole provider of forged wrought-iron bolts for the navy?

24. Besides the Blakely, what other two English guns were used by the Confederate Navy?

25. What gun constituted the forward armament of the CSS *Stonewall*?

19. Commander John M. Brooke.
20. An 8-inch Brooke pivot rifle forward, an 11-inch Brooke smooth-bore aft, and two 7-inch Brooke rifles in broadside.
21. Nine thousand pounds.
22. The Tredegar Iron Works at Richmond, Virginia.
23. The Naval Ordnance Works at Charlotte, North Carolina.
24. The Whitworth and the Armstrong.
25. A 300-pounder Armstrong rifle.

A Brooke rifle

This particular Brooke was used on the CSS *Tennessee*.

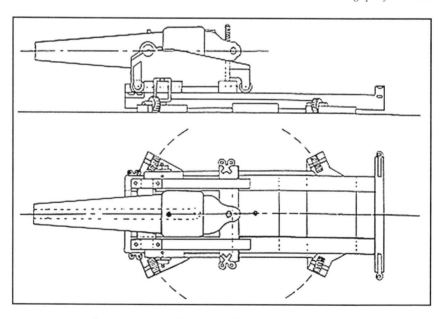

A drawing of a Brooke rifle on a pivot mount

One of two Blakely 7-inch rifles mounted on the CSS *Florida*

Author's Collection

Commander Catesby ap R. Jones

Naval Historical Center

Commander John M. Brooke

Naval Historical Center

Ruins of the Confederate Naval Gun Foundry at Selma,
Alabama, and an example of the machinery built there

John Ellis, Confederate Navy, Research Center, Mobile, Alabama

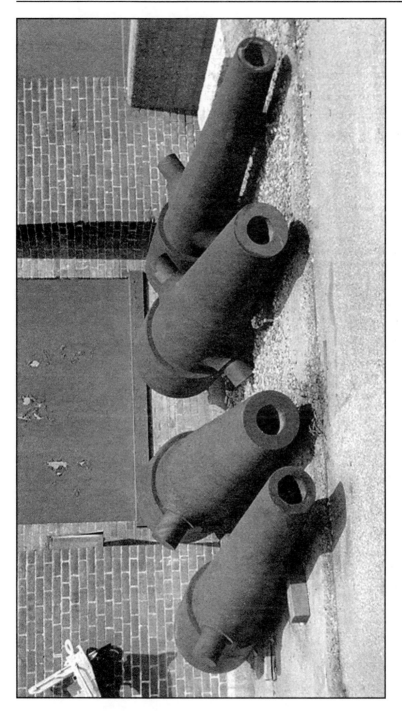

The four Brooke rifles from the ironclad CSS *Atlanta*

MEN AND OFFICERS

1. Who was the ranking officer of the Confederate Navy?
2. Name the only rear admiral in the Confederate Navy.
3. Approximately how many officers and men served in the Confederate Navy?
4. From what source were many of the men obtained who served on Confederate ironclads?
5. Roughly what percentage of officers resigned from the United States Navy and "went South" at the outbreak of the war?
6. What was a Confederate Navy recruiting station called?
7. What was the maximum number of enlisted personnel on duty with the Confederate Navy at any given time?
8. Name two nationalities found among the seamen that comprised the crew of the CSS *Alabama*.
9. In 1863, what was the monthly pay of a Confederate seaman?
10. In 1863, what was the annual pay of a Confederate captain who was on duty at sea?
11. Who was the executive officer of the cruiser CSS *Sumter* when she sailed out of New Orleans on June 30, 1861?
12. Name the nephew of President Davis who became a captain in the Confederate Navy.
13. Name the navy's very successful purchasing agent who was stationed in Europe throughout the war.
14. Who commanded the CSS *Florida* from May of 1862 until October of 1863?
15. What seaman served in the Army of Tennessee, transferred to the navy, and kept an extensive journal of his activities throughout the war?
16. What ration was served on Confederate ships, but was prohibited on Union vessels?
17. What navy officer with the rank of commander also received an appointment as a brigadier general in the Confederate Army?
18. Who commanded the CSS *Nashville* on her visit to England?

Men and Officers (ANSWERS)

1. Admiral Franklin Buchanan. He was the only full admiral in the Confederate Navy.

2. Rear Admiral Raphael Semmes. The former commander of the CSS *Alabama* was also given the rank of brigadier general in the army toward the end of the war.

3. About five thousand. Some historians put the figure closer to six thousand.

4. From the army.

5. Approximately 25 percent. Out of 1,550 total officers, 388 resigned. About the same number of Southern-born officers chose to remain in the Federal Navy.

6. A rendezvous. Stations were established in New Orleans, Savannah, Mobile, Raleigh, Norfolk, Macon, and Richmond.

7. There were 3,674 at the end of 1864.

8. English and Irish. There were also Dutch, Spanish, French, and Italians among the crew.

9. $22 per month.

10. $4,200 per year.

11. First Lieutenant John McIntosh Kell. The *Sumter*'s first lieutenant would also serve as Semmes' executive officer on the *Alabama* and later command an ironclad in the James River Squadron.

12. John Taylor Wood. An instructor at the U.S. Naval Academy, Wood was born in Minnesota of a Rhode Island father and a Louisiana mother. His wife was from Maryland.

13. Commander James D. Bulloch. Born near Savannah, Georgia, in 1823, Bulloch was from a distinguished Southern maritime family. He was also an uncle of President Theodore Roosevelt.

14. Commander John Newland Maffitt.

15. Seaman Robert Watson. His journal is one of the very few from an enlisted seaman to have survived the war.

16. The grog ration. Enlisted men were entitled to one gill of spirits or half-pint of wine per day.

17. Commander Richard L. Page. He commanded the outer defenses of Mobile Bay until the surrender of Fort Morgan on August 23, 1864.

18. Commander Robert B. Pegram.

19. Who was the chief naval constructor for the Confederate Navy?

20. What young naval officer led a raid into the harbor of Portsmouth, Maine, where he captured the U.S. revenue cutter *Caleb Cushing*?

21. Name the midshipman who wrote a history of the Confederate States Navy after the war.

22. Who was in command of the James River Squadron at the end of the war?

23. Name the midshipman who was killed in the attack and boarding of the USS *Underwriter*.

24. What was the minimum age for enlistment in the Confederate Navy?

25. From what state was First Lieutenant James I. Waddell, commander of the CSS *Shenandoah*?

26. Name the African American pilot that Confederates reported as killed in the attack on the USS *Water Witch*.

27. How were sailors called to battle stations?

28. What was a young boy called who was responsible for carrying powder to the guns?

29. While at sea, how did most of the Confederate cruisers add needed men to their crews?

30. Who was the Confederate Navy's ranking officer in Europe?

31. What was the equivalent army rank of a Confederate captain?

32. With what rank was a man with little or no seafaring experience enlisted?

33. What was the primary duty of a coal heaver?

34. What was meant by a "reefer"?

35. What Confederate captain became a rear admiral in the Peruvian navy after the war?

36. From what state was Admiral Franklin Buchanan?

37. What two men waged a bitter argument over who designed the CSS *Virginia*?

19. John L. Porter. The naval constructor from Portsmouth, Virginia, designed the CSS *Virginia* and most of the other ironclads built by the Confederacy.
20. First Lieutenant Charles W. Read. After towing the cutter out of the harbor, Read was forced to set her on fire when he was pursued by vengeful New England citizens.
21. J. Thomas Scharf.
22. Rear Admiral Raphael Semmes. The former commander of the *Alabama* had returned from England after his vessel had been sunk off Cherbourg, France, by the USS *Kearsarge*.
23. Passed Midshipman Palmer Sanders. The young Sanders had only recently been graduated from the Confederate Naval Academy.
24. Fourteen—with parents' consent.
25. North Carolina.
26. Moses Dallas. Instead of being killed, he evidently deserted to the enemy, for he later turned up in a Union Colored regiment.
27. By roll of the drum.
28. A powder monkey.
29. By enlisting volunteers from their captured prizes.
30. Captain Samuel Barron, Sr.
31. Colonel.
32. Landsman.
33. To shovel coal into the furnace beneath the boiler.
34. A sailor whose duties included deploying and taking in the sails.
35. Captain John R. Tucker. The former Confederate commanded a powerful combined fleet of Peru and Chile in their war against Spain.
36. Maryland. Buchanan's home was the "Rest" located on the banks of the Miles River on Maryland's Eastern Shore.
37. John L. Porter and John M. Brooke. Both men claimed that the design was his, when in reality they both probably contributed equally to the project.

38. Who was responsible for the restoration of the engines on the *Virginia*?

39. What army unit comprised approximately one-half of the crew of the CSS *Arkansas*?

40. Name the officer who commanded the Mosquito Fleet at the battle for Roanoke Island, North Carolina.

41. What bureau of the Navy Department was responsible for personnel?

42. What naval commander was dispatched to England specifically to arrange for the construction of ironclads?

43. What officer from the CSS *Sumter* was captured in Tangier, Morocco, and spirited off to prison in the United States?

44. Who was the naval captain in charge of one of the makeshift Confederate gunboats at the Battle of Galveston, Texas?

45. After the war, what former Confederate midshipman wrote *Recollections of a Rebel Reefer*?

46. Name the captain in the Confederate Navy who was a brother of General Robert E. Lee.

47. What was the highest rating that a petty officer could obtain?

48. Who was responsible for the maintenance of small arms aboard ship?

49. Who was the chief engineer of the CSS *Virginia* during the two-day battle in Hampton Roads?

50. What sailors were the last ones to salute the Confederate flag?

38. Engineer in Chief William P. Williamson. Williamson had been the engineer on the *Merrimack* and knew the engines well.

39. Three artillery companies from General M. Jeff Thompson's command.

40. Captain William F. Lynch.

41. The Office of Orders and Detail.

42. Commander James H. North. After much delay, North finally contracted with a builder in Glasgow, Scotland, to build a large armored warship. The ship was eventually sold, however, to the Danish government.

43. Paymaster Henry Myers. Mr. Turnstall, former U.S. Consular at Cadiz, Spain, volunteered to accompany Myers. Both men were illegally seized and sent to Fort Warren in Boston.

44. Lieutenant Leon Smith. A riverboat captain, a major in the army, Smith is not listed in the official register of Confederate naval officers, but there is a photograph in existence of him in the uniform of a Confederate Navy lieutenant.

45. Midshipman James Morris Morgan.

46. Captain Sidney Smith Lee was an older brother of Robert E. Lee.

47. Master's mate.

48. The armourer.

49. Chief Engineer J. Ashton Ramsay.

50. The crew of the CSS *Shenandoah* at Liverpool, England, on November 6, 1865.

**Admiral
Franklin Buchanan**

Naval Historical Center

**Rear Admiral
Raphael Semmes**

Naval Historical Center

**First Lieutenant John
McIntosh Kell**

Naval Historical Center

Captain John Taylor Wood

Naval Historical Center

**Chief Naval Constructor
John L. Porter**

Naval Historical Center

**First Lieutenant
Charles W. Read**

Nimitz Library, U.S. Naval Academy

**Commander John
Newland Maffitt**

John Ellis, Confederate Navy,
Research Center, Mobile, Alabama

**First Lieutenant
James I. Waddell**

Naval Historical Center

**Midshipman James
Morris Morgan**

Naval Historical Center

Captain Sidney Smith Lee

Library of Congress

The Navy on Land

1. Name the fortification on the James River seven miles below Richmond where navy gunners helped turn back attacking Union warships.

2. What navy commander was in charge of the combined army, navy, and marine forces at Drewry's Bluff when the Federals attacked on May 15, 1862?

3. At the time of the battle, from where were the six naval guns obtained that were mounted at Drewry's Bluff?

4. What Confederate crews manned the naval guns at the Battle of Drewry's Bluff?

5. Name the two Union ironclads that attacked Drewry's Bluff on May 15, 1862.

6. Who was the Confederate midshipman killed at the Battle of Drewry's Bluff?

7. Name the Confederate Navy captain who was taken captive with the fall of Fort Hatteras on the North Carolina Outer Banks, August 29, 1861.

8. What ship was the crew from that manned the land fortifications when Union warships attacked and destroyed the Mosquito Fleet at Elizabeth City, North Carolina?

9. Name the battery south of Fort Fisher that guarded the entrance to Wilmington, North Carolina, and was manned by Confederate sailors.

10. What naval officer commanded this battery during the battle for Fort Fisher, January 13–15, 1865?

11. On the first attack on Fort Fisher, December 24, 1864, what naval crew manned several of the Brooke guns on the sea face wall?

12. In September of 1862, what naval crew was stationed in the fortifications at Port Hudson, Louisiana, overlooking the Mississippi River?

13. What inland city in North Carolina was selected for development of a large naval facility?

14. Name two items produced by the Charlotte Navy Yard.

THE NAVY ON LAND (ANSWERS)

1. Drewry's Bluff. The Federals named the fortification on the bluff overlooking the James River, "Fort Darling." Union ironclads were stopped there by Confederate fire on May 15, 1862.

2. Commander Ebenezer Farrand.

3. From the CSS *Jamestown*, which had been deliberately sunk as an obstruction, and from the CSS *Patrick Henry*.

4. Men from the CSS *Virginia* and the CSS *Jamestown*.

5. The USS *Galena* and the USS *Monitor*.

6. Midshipman Daniel Carroll.

7. Captain Samuel R. Barron, Sr. Barron had arrived the previous night, and was asked by the exhausted army commander to take command of the garrison.

8. The CSS *Beaufort* commanded by Lieutenant William H. Parker. The *Beaufort* escaped to Norfolk via the Dismal Swamp Canal.

9. Battery Buchanan.

10. First Lieutenant Robert F. Chapman.

11. The crew from the CSS *Chickamauga*.

12. Sailors from the CSS *Arkansas*, which they had been forced to destroy near Baton Rouge the previous month. On September 7, 1862, they caused extensive damage to the Federal ironclad USS *Essex* when she attempted to run past their guns.

13. Charlotte, North Carolina.

14. Gun carriages and wrought-iron projectiles for heavy cannon.

15. Who commanded the Charlotte Navy Yard from 1864 to the end of the war?

16. Where was the Confederate Naval Iron Works located?

17. When Richmond was evacuated in April of 1865, who commanded the naval brigade that joined in the retreat to Appomattox?

18. From which three cities had most of the men been stationed who formed this naval brigade?

19. In what final battle did the naval brigade put up a vigorous fight?

20. What Confederate midshipman refused to surrender at Sayler's Creek, escaped, and became a staff officer for his brother, Major General Fitzhugh Lee?

21. What was unique about three sailors from the ironclad CSS *Chicora* who surrendered with Lee's army at Appomattox?

22. Upon the evacuation of Richmond, what group of men constituted the Semmes naval brigade?

23. What mode of transportation did the Semmes naval brigade utilize in leaving Richmond?

24. What was the destination of the Semmes naval brigade when they left Richmond?

25. When did the Semmes naval brigade finally surrender?

15. Chief Engineer H. Ashton Ramsay.

16. Columbus, Georgia.

17. Captain John R. Tucker.

18. From the Charleston, Savannah, and Wilmington stations. These areas had been evacuated upon the approach of General Sherman's army from the south.

19. The Battle of Sayler's Creek, Virginia, on April 6, 1865. The army troops had been captured, and the naval brigade, although surrounded by the enemy, charged the astonished Federals and refused to surrender.

20. Midshipman Daniel M. Lee.

21. They were African American. Their names were: Charles Cleapor, Joseph Johnson, and J. Heck.

22. Men from the James River Squadron.

23. By train.

24. Danville, Virginia.

25. On May 1, 1865. Raphael Semmes had received orders for his brigade to join with General Joseph E. Johnston in North Carolina, but when he arrived he found that Johnston and the Army of Tennessee had surrendered to General Sherman.

Bird's-eye view of the Battle of Drewry's Bluff

Battles and Leaders

Commander Ebenezer Farrand
Alabama Archives

**First Lieutenant
Robert F. Chapman**
Naval Historical Center

**Chief Engineer
H. Ashton Ramsay**
Author's Collection

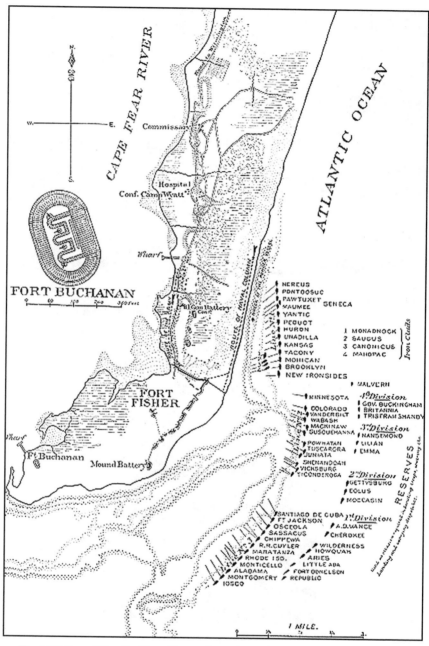

Fort Fisher, North Carolina, showing the position of Battery Buchanan which was manned by Confederate sailors

Battles and Leaders

Captain John R. Tucker

Scharf: *History of the Confederate States Navy*

**Midshipman
Daniel M. Lee**

Courtesy of William A. Turner

The Confederate States Marine Corps

1. When was the Confederate Marine Corps established?

2. What officer served as commandant of the Marine Corps throughout the entire war?

3. The commandant of the Marine Corps hailed from what state?

4. What was the term of enlistment for a Confederate Marine?

5. What was the largest number of Marines under arms at any one time?

6. Name the brother-in-law of Jefferson Davis who was a lieutenant in the Marine Corps.

7. Where was the focal point of Marine Corps activity in the first few months of the war?

8. Name the second in command of the Confederate Marine Corps.

9. What Marine company served on the CSS *Virginia*?

10. How many Marines served on the *Virginia* during the two-day battle of Hampton Roads?

11. Name the island off the coast of Mississippi that was occupied and defended by Confederate Marines in July of 1861.

12. How many men constituted the Marine guard on the cruiser CSS *Sumter*?

13. In what famous battle on May 15, 1862, did the Marines play a significant role?

14. Where was the permanent base for the Marines finally established.

15. Name the Confederate fort near Mobile, Alabama, that was staunchly defended in part by Marines on April 9, 1865.

16. What name was given to the home base of the Marines?

17. At Charleston, what Federal night attack did a company of Marines who were stationed on the CSS *Chicora* help repulse?

18. How many Marines were involved in the Confederate night attack and capture of the USS *Underwriter*?

THE CONFEDERATE STATES MARINE CORPS (ANSWERS)

1. On March 16, 1861, by an act of the Confederate Congress.
2. Colonel Lloyd J. Beall.
3. Maryland.
4. Four years.
5. Five hundred seventy-one as of October 31, 1864.
6. First Lieutenant Becket K. Howell. The lieutenant's sister, Varina Howell, was the wife of Jefferson Davis.
7. Pensacola, Florida. Over three hundred Marines, forming three companies, were stationed there by the summer of 1861.
8. Lieutenant Colonel Henry B. Tyler.
9. Captain Reuben T. Thom's Company C.
10. Fifty-four. Several of the *Virginia's* guns were served by Marines.
11. Ship Island. The island was attacked by the USS *Massachusetts* on July 9, but she was forced to withdraw under heavy fire from the Marines.
12. Twenty men under the command of First Lieutenant Becket K. Howell.
13. The Battle of Drewry's Bluff. The Marines lined the riverbank on both sides and poured their rifle fire into the open ports of the Union ironclads causing many carnalities.
14. At Drewry's Bluff, Virginia.
15. Fort Blakely, Alabama.
16. Camp Beall at Drewry's Bluff.
17. The Union boat attack on Fort Sumter, September 8–9, 1863. Approximately two dozen U.S. Marines were killed, wounded, or captured.
18. Twenty-five C.S. Marines led by Captain Thomas S. Wilson. One Marine was killed and four wounded.

19. Who commanded the Marine guard on the ironclad CSS *Raleigh*?

20. At the Battle of Mobile Bay on August 5, 1864, how many Marines helped serve the guns on the CSS *Tennessee*?

21. Name two other Confederate warships of the Mobile Squadron that included Marines on board.

22. What was the total number of Marine casualties in the battle for Fort Fisher, January 13–15, 1865?

23. Who commanded the Marine contingent that accompanied navy Lieutenant Charles W. Read's overland expedition around Grant's army in February of 1865?

24. How many Marines surrendered with Lee's army at Appomattox?

25. Who were the last Confederate Marines to surrender?

19. Second Lieutenant Henry M. Doak.
20. Thirty-five Marines commanded by First Lieutenant David G. Raney.
21. The CSS *Morgan* (15), and the CSS *Gaines* (17).
22. Between 25 and 30 were unaccounted for and presumed killed in action. Sixty-six were made prisoners, 10 of whom were wounded, three mortally.
23. First Lieutenant James Thurston.
24. Twenty-five—four officers and 21 enlisted men.
25. The Marine guard of the CSS *Shenandoah*, Liverpool, England, November 6, 1865.

**Colonel Lloyd J. Beall,
CSMC**

Scharf: *History of the Confederate States Navy*

**Lieutenant Becket K.
Howell, CSMC**

Sinclair: *Two Years on the Alabama*

The Confederate Marine Corps camp at Drewry's Bluff

Illustrated London News, November 15, 1862

Night attack on the USS *Underwriter* involving Confederate Marines

The Confederate Soldier in the Civil War

THE CONFEDERATE NAVAL ACADEMY

1. When did the Confederate Naval Academy begin operations?

2. Where was the naval academy located?

3. What naval bureau in Richmond administered the naval academy?

4. Where were the alterations made to the *Patrick Henry* to convert her into a school ship?

5. Name the Confederate officer in the Navy Department who had overall responsibility for the naval school.

6. Who did Secretary Mallory appoint as superintendent and commandant of the school?

7. What was the name of the textbook written by Parker outlining the regulations of the academy?

8. In the fall of 1863, how many midshipmen constituted the first class at the academy?

9. When the school opened, who was the commandant of midshipmen?

10. How many classes did the academy graduate?

11. Before being converted into the school ship, in what famous battle had the *Patrick Henry* participated?

12. Name three instructors who taught at the Confederate Naval Academy.

13. Where were the recitation rooms located where classes were held?

14. How were midshipmen appointed to the naval school?

15. What was the general age range of the students at the academy?

16. What activities kept interrupting the midshipmen's studies as the war progressed?

17. How many midshipmen from the academy participated in the night attack on the USS *Underwriter*?

18. Name the midshipman who was killed in the attack on the USS *Underwriter*.

THE CONFEDERATE NAVAL ACADEMY (ANSWERS)

1. In August of 1863.
2. On the school ship CSS *Patrick Henry* at Drewry's Bluff on the James River.
3. The Office of Ordnance and Hydrography.
4. At the naval facility at Rocketts Landing, Richmond, Virginia.
5. Commander John M. Brooke. Brooke was in charge of the Office of Ordnance and Hydrography.
6. First Lieutenant William H. Parker. A former professor at the U.S. Naval Academy in Annapolis, Parker was serving at the time as the executive officer on the ironclad CSS *Palmetto State* at Charleston.
7. *Regulations for the Interior Police of the Confederate States School-Ship Patrick Henry.*
8. Fifty-two.
9. First Lieutenant Benjamin P. Loyall.
10. Basically three—fall of 1863, spring and fall of 1864. The spring class of 1865 never really had an opportunity to be graduated.
11. The two-day Battle of Hampton Roads, March 8–9, 1862.
12. First Lieutenant Oscar F. Johnston, professor of astronomy, navigation, and surveying; First Lieutenant Charles J. Graves, instructor in seamanship; and Second Lieutenant William V. Comstock, instructor in gunnery.
13. On board the *Patrick Henry*.
14. By members of Congress from their respective districts, or by the president from the Confederacy at large.
15. Fourteen to 17 years of age.
16. The pressing need for additional men to man the batteries along the James River, and to supplement the crews of the ironclads.
17. Eight—William F. Clayton, Henry S. Cooke, Paul H. Gibbs, Daniel M. Lee, John B. Northrop, Palmer Saunders, J. Thomas Scharf, and Richard C. Slaughter.
18. Midshipman Palmer Saunders.

19. What was the title of the textbook written by Parker that became the standard manual for the academy?

20. On May 10, 1864, how many students from the academy were temporarily transferred to the ships of the James River Squadron?

21. Where was Midshipman James Morris Morgan assigned after he was graduated in October of 1864?

22. How many newly graduated midshipmen from the naval academy served on the ironclads of the James River Squadron during the Battle of Trent's Reach?

23. Near the end of the war, what final duty fell to the lot of the midshipmen from the naval academy?

24. Upon the evacuation of Richmond, what was the fate of the school ship *Patrick Henry*?

25. Where did the corps of midshipmen finally disband?

19. *Elements of Seamanship*, published in Richmond, May 1864.
20. Nineteen.
21. To Battery Semmes on the James River.
22. Ten.
23. They were detailed to guard the gold from the Confederate Treasury as it was evacuated to the south.
24. The *Patrick Henry* was burned near Rocketts Landing at Richmond.
25. Abbeville, South Carolina (May 2, 1865).

The Confederate Naval Academy's school ship, CSS *Patrick Henry*

Official Records Navy

**First Lieutenant
William H. Parker**

Scharf: *History of the Confederate States Navy*

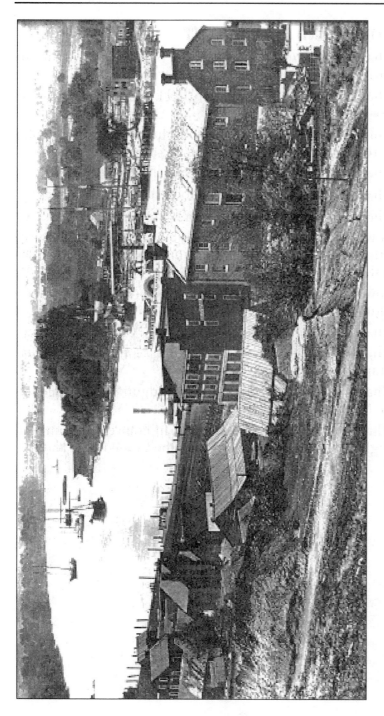

Rocketts Landing in the foreground with the
Confederate Navy Yard across the river

Uniforms and Equipment

1. What color were most Confederate officers' navy uniforms during the first two years of the war?
2. What color was the regulation frock coat for Confederate naval officers?
3. While army regulations called for blue trousers, what color were navy trousers supposed to be?
4. What color were the hats of the enlisted personnel?
5. What was each sailor required to wear around his neck?
6. Where was the navy's only shoe factory located?
7. How did the method of displaying a Confederate naval officer's insignia of rank differ from that of his counterpart in the army?
8. How many different sizes of buttons adorned an officer's regulation coat?
9. What was the official shoulder arm of the Confederate Navy?
10. What was the background color of a sea officer's shoulder strap?
11. What was the most widely used handgun in the Confederate Navy?
12. What handgun was manufactured in France, Belgium, and England, and used extensively in the Confederate Navy?
13. How many stars adorned a flag officer's or admiral's shoulder strap?
14. Because of a shortage of gray cloth, what clothing was often substituted for regulation uniforms?
15. How many gold stripes were embroidered on the sleeve of a flag officer or admiral?
16. Instead of gold lace, what did Confederate midshipmen have on their sleeves?
17. What shoulder insignia identified a Confederate States Marine Corps officer?
18. What was the most common rifle issued to Confederate Marines?

UNIFORMS AND EQUIPMENT (ANSWERS)

1. Navy blue. Most officers continued to wear their blue Federal uniforms during the first part of the war, the switch to gray being very unpopular.
2. Steel gray.
3. Steel gray, except in summer when they could be white.
4. Black. White hats could be worn in summer.
5. A black silk neckerchief.
6. Graniteville, South Carolina. This facility was soon taken over by the army causing most navy shoes to be imported from England.
7. The navy utilized shoulder straps whereas the army's rank was displayed on a stand-up collar.
8. Three.
9. Carbines. These included the two-band Enfield rifle (Model 1858 short Enfield), the 1st Model Maynard rifle (carbine), and the short Whitney-Enfield rifle.
10. Sky-blue. The regulations called for a strip of "sky-blue cloth, edged in black, four inches long and one and three-eighths wide, bordered with an embroidery of gold one-quarter of an inch in width..."
11. The five-shot Kerr revolver (.44 caliber), made by the London Armoury.
12. The LeMat revolver. Approximately three thousand were shipped to the Confederacy, most of which were paid for by the Navy Department. Those not needed were transferred to the army and the cavalry.
13. Four stars of gold embroidery.
14. Civilian clothing as worn by those in the merchant marine.
15. Four, the top stripe having a single loop three inches high.
16. Three medium-sized navy buttons.
17. A four-cord shoulder knot similar to that worn by U.S. Marine officers.
18. The .577-caliber British Enfield.

19. What item was to be worn on the sleeve of all petty officers?
20. Although obsolete, what weapon was sometimes retained as part of a Confederate sailor's equipment?
21. What navy cutlass was copied by several Southern manufacturers?
22. What uniform markings designated a Confederate Navy surgeon?
23. The regulations prescribed for how many large buttons on the front of a sea officer's frock coat?
24. What type of hat, in lieu of the regulation navy gray, were officers permitted to wear during the summer?
25. What color were all Confederate Navy shoes and boots required to be?
26. What color never entirely disappeared from the ranks of Confederate sailors?
27. How many shoulder stars and sleeve stripes designated a Confederate Navy captain?
28. What shoulder insignia designated a Confederate passed midshipman?

19. A foul anchor embroidered in black silk on gray jackets. The same anchor was to be embroidered in blue silk on summer white frocks.

20. Boarding pikes.

21. The 1841 U.S. Navy model cutlass.

22. Shoulder straps of black cloth with two sprigs of crossed olive branches embroidered in gold.

23. Eighteen—two rows of nine each.

24. White straw hats.

25. Black.

26. Navy blue.

27. Three stars and three sleeve stripes.

28. A strip of gold lace four inches long and one-half inch wide.

The officers of the CSS *Sumter* photographed the day before the cruiser sailed from New Orleans. Note the blue uniforms with Confederate cuff markings.

Naval Historical Center

**Joseph N. Barney,
wearing the proper
uniform of a commander
in the Confederate Navy**

Author's Collection

Captain Raphael Semmes *(foreground),*
and his first lieutenant, John M. Kell

This photograph, taken on the *Alabama* while visiting South Africa, confirms that
both officers had now switched to the regulation gray uniform.

**A group of Confederate sailors believed to be
the crew from the CSS *Atlanta***

INVENTORS, DESIGNERS, AND SHIPBUILDERS

1. Who is generally credited with inventing the spar torpedo which was mounted on numerous Confederate torpedo boats and ironclads?

2. Name the individual responsible for the building of the ironclad CSS *Albemarle*.

3. Name the designer and builder of the torpedo boat CSS *St. Patrick*.

4. What Southern inventor experimented with underwater explosives in his cousin's bathtub in Richmond, Virginia?

5. What Confederate Navy lieutenant was responsible for developing the electrically fired torpedo into a very successful and technologically advanced state?

6. What young army captain developed a very successful chemical fuse that could be used to detonate torpedoes?

7. Name the two brothers who designed and nearly completed the huge ironclad CSS *Mississippi*.

8. Who was the naval constructor who designed the majority of the gunboats and ironclads for the Confederate Navy?

9. What naval commander drew the plans for the commerce raider CSS *Alabama*?

10. Who was the builder of the *Alabama*?

11. Name the French builder who was responsible for the construction of the armored ram CSS *Stonewall*.

12. Name the naval constructor in Richmond who designed the Squib class torpedo boats of the James River Squadron.

13. What Confederate naval officer, through experiments, determined the best slant angle for iron armor on warships?

14. Who were the designers and builders of the world's first successful submarine, the CSS *H. L. Hunley*?

15. Name the designer and builder of the torpedo boat CSS *David*.

16. What two men both claimed primary responsibility for designing the ironclad CSS *Virginia*?

17. Where were the majority of blockade runners constructed?

Inventors, Designers, and Shipbuilders (Answers)

1. Captain Francis D. Lee, CSA.
2. Gilbert Elliott. Born in Elizabeth City, North Carolina, young Elliott was only 18 years of age when he contracted with the Confederate government to build the *Albemarle*.
3. John P. Halligan at Selma, Alabama.
4. Matthew Fontaine Maury.
5. Hunter Davidson. When Commander Matthew F. Maury was transferred to Europe, Davidson assumed command of the Torpedo Bureau.
6. Francis D. Lee.
7. Asa and Nelson Tift. The *Mississippi* had to be destroyed when the Union Navy passed the forts below New Orleans in April of 1862.
8. Chief Naval Constructor John L. Porter.
9. Commander James D. Bulloch.
10. John Laird & Sons of Birkenhead, England.
11. Lucien Arman. The *Stonewall* was the only European ironclad actually to be delivered to the Confederate Navy; however, she arrived in Cuba after the war had ended.
12. William A. Graves.
13. Commander John M. Brooke.
14. James R. McClintock and Baxter Watson.
15. David C. Ebaugh.
16. John L. Porter and John M. Brooke.
17. England. A large percentage were built in Scotland as well.

18. Name the shipbuilder who constructed the ironclad CSS *Tennessee*.

19. Who was the Confederate naval officer who designed an exceptionally powerful naval gun?

20. Name the original builder of the CSS *Arkansas*.

21. Who was the naval officer who oversaw the completion of the *Arkansas*?

22. Who was the designer of the floating battery CSS *Georgia*?

23. Name the designer of the ironclads CSS *Charleston* and CSS *Virginia II*.

24. Who was the designer and builder of two submarines constructed at the Tredegar Iron Works in Richmond, Virginia?

25. Name the Confederate officer who succeeded in finishing the construction of the ironclad CSS *Missouri*.

26. Who was the builder of the cruiser CSS *Florida*?

27. Name the designer of the Confederate gunboat CSS *Chattahoochee*.

28. Who was the builder of the ironclad CSS *Savannah*?

18. Henry D. Bassett.

19. Commander John M. Brooke. Brooke's 7-inch and 6.4-inch rifles became the main armament of most Confederate ironclads.

20. John T. Shirley of Memphis, Tennessee.

21. Commander Isaac N. Brown.

22. A. N. Miller, a Savannah foundryman with little or no experience in naval architecture.

23. Naval Constructor William A. Graves.

24. William Cheeney.

25. Lieutenant Jonathan H. Carter. Carter became the commander of the *Missouri* when she was commissioned at Shreveport, Louisiana, on September 12, 1863.

26. William C. Miller & Sons of Liverpool, England.

27. Chief Engineer James H. Warner.

28. Henry F. Willink, Jr., a second generation shipbuilder from Savannah, Georgia.

Gilbert Elliott, builder of the CSS *Albemarle*

Commander John M. Brooke in later years

The CSS *Virginia* nearing completion in the granite dry dock at the Gosport Navy Yard

Battles and Leaders

Commander Isaac N. Brown

Scharf: *History of the Confederate States Navy*

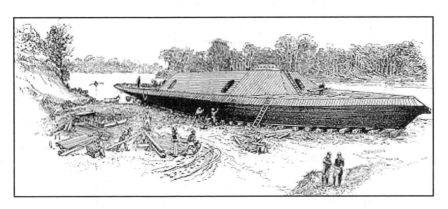

**The CSS *Albemarle* under construction on the
bank of the Roanoke River**

Battles and Leaders

ENGAGEMENTS AND BATTLES

1. Name the first battle between two armored warships.
2. What was the date of this battle?
3. Name the two Union warships destroyed by the CSS *Virginia* on the first day of the battle at Hampton Roads.
4. What method of attack was used by the *Virginia* to sink the *Cumberland*?
5. How did the *Virginia* destroy the *Congress*?
6. What caused the Confederate gunboat CSS *Beaufort* to cease her rescue operation of Union sailors from the burning *Congress*?
7. What was the number of Federal casualties in the first day's fighting at Hampton Roads?
8. How many Confederate casualties were sustained during the first day at Hampton Roads?
9. Name the famous Union ironclad that was encountered by the *Virginia* on the second day's battle at Hampton Roads.
10. What was the *Virginia*'s original intention on the second day (March 9) at Hampton Roads?
11. Name two things that prevented the *Virginia* from defeating the *Monitor*.
12. Which vessel, the *Virginia* or the *Monitor*, do most historians consider as the victor in this historic battle?
13. What strategic island in the sounds of North Carolina fell to the Federals on February 8, 1862?
14. How many Confederate vessels were involved in the battle for this island?
15. How was the attack on Roanoke Island referred to in the North?
16. How many Federal vessels were involved in the attack on Roanoke Island?
17. What term did the Confederate's use to describe their tiny squadron?
18. Who commanded the Confederate squadron at the Battle of Roanoke Island?

ENGAGEMENTS AND BATTLES (ANSWERS)

1. The Battle of Hampton Roads.
2. March 8 and 9, 1862.
3. The USS *Cumberland* and the USS *Congress.*
4. The *Virginia* rammed the *Cumberland* and set her ablaze by gunfire.
5. She set her on fire by the use of hot shot (solid shot heated red-hot in a furnace). The *Congress* exploded later that night when the flames reached her magazine.
6. Federal soldiers opened fire on the CSS *Beaufort* from the shoreline.
7. Approximately 325. The *Cumberland* listed 121 known killed and 30 wounded, while the best estimates from the *Congress* were 110 dead and 26 wounded, 10 of whom later died. The USS *Minnesota* had two or three killed and nine wounded. The remainder of the Federal casualties were from the batteries on shore.
8. Twenty-seven. The *Virginia* had two killed and eight wounded. The *Beaufort* and *Raleigh* between them had 10 casualties, and seven occurred on the *Patrick Henry.*
9. The USS *Monitor.*
10. The destruction of the USS *Minnesota.*
11. She was slower and could not ram her, and she carried no solid shot which might have penetrated the *Monitor.*
12. Neither one. Most consider the battle a draw.
13. Roanoke Island.
14. Nine. They included the CSS *Seabird*, the CSS *Curlew*, the CSS *Ellis*, the CSS *Beaufort*, the CSS *Raleigh*, the CSS *Forrest*, the CSS *Fanny*, the CSS *Appomattox*, and the schooner CSS *Black Warrior.*
15. The Burnside Expedition.
16. Twenty navy ships plus numerous army gunboats.
17. The Mosquito Fleet.
18. Captain William F. Lynch.

19. After the loss of Roanoke Island, where did the Mosquito Fleet fight its final battle?

20. Which Confederate vessel was the only one to escape at the Battle of Elizabeth City?

21. Name the U.S. warship that was sunk by the CSS *Alabama* off the coast of Galveston, Texas.

22. How long did it take the *Alabama* to sink the *Hatteras*?

23. How many men from the *Hatteras* did the *Alabama* manage to rescue?

24. Where was the battle between the CSS *Alabama* and the USS *Kearsarge*?

25. What date was the battle between the *Alabama* and the *Kearsarge*?

26. What advantage did the *Kearsarge* have that Semmes claimed he had no knowledge of?

27. What disadvantage worked heavily against the *Alabama*?

28. What shot did the *Alabama*'s gunners succeed in making that came close to destroying the *Kearsarge*?

29. How long did the battle last?

30. As the *Alabama* was sinking, what vessel came to the rescue of many of the cruiser's men?

31. How many Confederate casualties were sustained during the battle?

32. What Union warship was sunk by the Confederate ironclad CSS *Albemarle*?

33. In what battle and in what place did this sinking take place?

34. How did the *Albemarle* sink the *Southfield*?

35. Name the other Union vessel that fought the *Albemarle* at the Battle of Plymouth.

36. Who was the commander of the *Albemarle* in this battle?

37. What was his intention when he steamed the *Albemarle* into Albemarle Sound on May 5, 1864?

38. Name the three principal Federal warships that battled the *Albemarle* in Albemarle Sound.

39. Name the other two vessels that had accompanied the Confederate ironclad into Albemarle Sound.

19. Elizabeth City, North Carolina.
20. The CSS *Raleigh*.
21. The USS *Hatteras*.
22. Thirteen minutes.
23. One hundred eighteen. Two Federal sailors were killed and five were wounded in the battle. Six men escaped to the Federal fleet in a boat.
24. Off the coast of Cherbourg, France.
25. June 19, 1864.
26. Chain armor. The *Kearsarge* had heavy anchor chains draped over her sides which were enclosed by planking.
27. Much of her ammunition, which was more than two years old, was defective.
28. They lodged a shell in the sternpost of the *Kearsarge*; it failed to explode.
29. One hour, twenty minutes.
30. The English yacht *Deerhound*.
31. Forty-two. Nine men were killed and 21 listed as wounded. Twelve men were lost by drowning when the ship went down. One hundred twenty-seven men were rescued.
32. The USS *Southfield*.
33. The battle for Plymouth, North Carolina, April 18, 1864.
34. By ramming.
35. The USS *Miami*.
36. Commander James W. Cooke. The *Albemarle*'s captain was from North Carolina and had previously participated in the fighting for Roanoke Island where he was wounded and taken prisoner.
37. Cooke was intent on joining forces with the ironclad CSS *Neuse* for an attack on New Bern, North Carolina.
38. The USS *Mattabesett*, the USS *Wyalusing*, and the USS *Sassacus*.
39. The CSS *Bombshell* and the CSS *Cotton Plant*.

40. What was the total number of Federal vessels faced by the *Albemarle* in the Battle of Albemarle Sound?

41. Name the Confederate vessel that was captured in the Battle of Albemarle Sound.

42. What was unique about one of the powder boys on the *Albemarle*?

43. Name the Union warship that crashed into the *Albemarle*.

44. What finally ended the Battle of Albemarle Sound?

45. Name the uncompleted Confederate ironclad that fought Admiral Farragut's fleet at the Battle of New Orleans.

46. Who was the overall Confederate naval commander at the Battle of New Orleans?

47. On what date was the Battle of New Orleans fought?

48. How many Federal warships successfully passed the forts below New Orleans and defeated the defending Confederate ships?

49. How many Confederate warships escaped destruction at the Battle of New Orleans?

50. What Confederate ironclad fought two Federal fleets simultaneously on the Mississippi River?

51. During her short life, in how many separate battles was the CSS *Arkansas* involved before her destruction?

52. How many Confederate casualties were sustained by the crew of the *Arkansas* during her passage to Vicksburg?

53. What were Union casualties during this battle?

54. Name the island in the Mississippi River near the Kentucky-Tennessee state line that was defended in part by ships of the Confederate Navy.

55. When was the naval Battle of Memphis fought?

56. How many Confederate vessels were lost in this battle?

57. When was the engagement between the ironclad CSS *Raleigh* and three Union warships, off the mouth of the Cape Fear River?

58. Who commanded the *Raleigh* in this attack on the Federal fleet?

40. Eight.

41. The CSS *Bombshell.*

42. Benjamin H. Gray, a lad of 12 years of age, was African American.

43. The USS *Sassacus.*

44. A shot from the *Albemarle* exploded the boiler of the *Sassacus.*

45. The CSS *Louisiana.*

46. Commander John K. Mitchell.

47. April 24, 1862.

48. Thirteen. One Union ship, the USS *Varuna,* had been sunk by the Louisiana state gunboat *Governor Moore.*

49. None. Several vessels, including the *Louisiana,* were destroyed by their own crews to prevent capture.

50. The CSS *Arkansas.*

51. Five.

52. Twenty-five. Ten were killed and 15 wounded.

53. One hundred eleven. Forty-two Federal sailors were killed and 69 were wounded.

54. Island No. 10.

55. June 6, 1862.

56. Seven. Only the CSS *General Earl Van Dorn* escaped.

57. May 6, 1864.

58. First Lieutenant J. Pembroke Jones.

59. Name the two small Confederate gunboats that accompanied the *Raleigh* in this attack.

60. On what date was the Battle of Trent's Reach, Virginia?

61. Name the three Confederate ironclads involved in the Battle of Trent's Reach.

62. What Union ironclad pounded two of the Confederate ironclads?

63. Name the commanders of the three Confederate ironclads at the Battle of Trent's Reach.

64. What Confederate gunboat exploded when a shell reached her magazine in the Trent's Reach battle?

65. Name the Union monitor whose 15-inch gunfire forced the Confederate ironclad CSS *Atlanta* to surrender.

66. Where and when did this engagement between the *Atlanta* and the Federal monitor take place?

67. Why was the *Atlanta* forced to surrender?

68. Who was in command of the *Atlanta* at the time of her surrender?

69. What occurred at Charleston, South Carolina, on January 30, 1863?

70. Name the two Confederate ironclads that attacked the Federal blockading fleet off Charleston.

71. Who were the commanders of the two Confederate ironclads?

72. What Union warship was rammed by the *Palmetto State* causing the Federal to surrender?

73. What Union vessel was attacked by the *Chicora*?

74. How long did the break in the blockade last?

75. When did the Battle of Galveston take place?

76. Name the two Confederate vessels involved in the retaking of Galveston.

77. What Union vessel was boarded and captured at the Battle of Galveston?

78. What were Confederate casualties in the retaking of Galveston?

59. The CSS *Yadkin* and the CSS *Equator*.

60. January 23–24, 1865.

61. The CSS *Virginia II*, the CSS *Richmond*, and the CSS *Fredericksburg*.

62. The USS *Onondaga*. The *Onondaga*'s massive 15-inch gun was particularly devastating against the armor of the *Virginia II*.

63. Lieutenant John W. Dunnington (*Virginia II*), Commander John M. Kell (*Richmond*), and Lieutenant Francis E. Shepperd (*Fredericksburg*).

64. The CSS *Drewry*. Fortunately, the officers and crew had just been moved into protective confines of the CSS *Richmond*'s casemate.

65. The USS *Weehawken*.

66. In Wassaw Sound, Georgia, on June 17, 1863.

67. She had run aground, and with her deck tilted, could not bring her guns to bear.

68. Commander William A. Webb.

69. Two Confederate warships temporarily broke the blockade.

70. The CSS *Chicora* and the CSS *Palmetto State*.

71. First Lieutenant John Rutledge commanded the *Palmetto State*, and Commander John R. Tucker was skipper of the *Chicora*.

72. The USS *Mercedita*.

73. The USS *Keystone State*.

74. Twenty-four hours. By the next day, the Union vessels had returned.

75. January 1, 1863.

76. The CSS *Bayou City* and the CSS *Neptune*.

77. The USS *Harriet Lane*. The *Harriet Lane* was repaired and commissioned into Confederate service as the CSS *Harriet Lane*.

78. Twenty-seven were killed and more than one hundred were wounded.

79. Name the former executive officer of the CSS *Arkansas* who was killed in the engagement between the *J. A. Cotton* and several Union warships on the Teche Bayou in Louisiana.

80. What Federal officer, the brother of a high-ranking Confederate naval officer, was killed in the engagement on the Teche Bayou?

81. What Confederate cruiser ran the blockade in broad daylight into Mobile, Alabama?

82. What was the name of the Federal blockader that attempted to prevent the CSS *Florida* from entering Mobile, Alabama?

83. Why did the Florida not open fire on the Union blockaders?

84. When did the *Florida* escape from Mobile?

85. What Federal warship chased the *Florida* through the night of the 16th and all the next day?

86. Upon their return to Wilmington, North Carolina, what two Confederate cruisers had running gun battles with Federal blockaders?

87. On what date was the Battle of Mobile Bay?

88. How many Confederate warships were engaged in the Battle of Mobile Bay?

89. Who was the Confederate commander of the Mobile Squadron?

90. Upon what warship did the squadron commander fly his flag?

91. Name the commander of the CSS *Tennessee*.

92. What Union monitor was sunk by a Confederate torpedo at the Battle of Mobile Bay?

93. Who was the commander of the Union fleet that forced its way into Mobile Bay?

94. Name the Confederate naval surgeon who tended to the wounded Franklin Buchanan.

95. Of the 114 officers and men of the Union ironclad *Tecumseh*, how many survived when she went down?

96. Name two of the Union warships that rammed the *Tennessee*.

79. Lieutenant Henry K. Stevens.

80. Lieutenant Commander Thomas M. Buchanan, brother of Admiral Franklin Buchanan of the Confederate Navy.

81. The CSS *Florida* on September 4, 1862.

82. The USS *Oneida*.

83. Most of her crew were sick with yellow fever, and certain necessary parts for the guns were missing.

84. January 16, 1863.

85. The USS *R. R. Cuyler*. The 10-gun Union ship lost the *Florida* in the darkness of the following night.

86. The CSS *Chickamauga* and the CSS *Tallahassee*.

87. August 5, 1864.

88. Four. The ironclad CSS *Tennessee*, and the gunboats CSS *Gaines*, CSS *Morgan*, and CSS *Selma*.

89. Admiral Franklin Buchanan.

90. The CSS *Tennessee*.

91. Commander James D. Johnston.

92. The USS *Tecumseh*.

93. Admiral David G. Farragut.

94. Surgeon Daniel B. Conrad.

95. Twenty-one.

96. The USS *Monongahela* and the USS *Lackawanna*.

97. What was the primary damage that forced the *Tennessee* to surrender?

98. What was the nature of Admiral Buchanan's wound?

99. How long had the Battle of Mobile Bay lasted?

100. When was the last shot of the war fired by the Confederate Navy?

97. Her rudder chains were shot away and she could not maneuver.
98. A broken leg.
99. More than four hours.
100. June 27, 1865, by the CSS *Shenandoah* in the Arctic Ocean.

Captain William F. Lynch

He was the commander of Confederate naval forces at the Battle of Roanoke Island, February 8, 1862.

Courtesy of William A. Turner

Captain James W. Cooke

Scharf: *History of the Confederate States Navy*

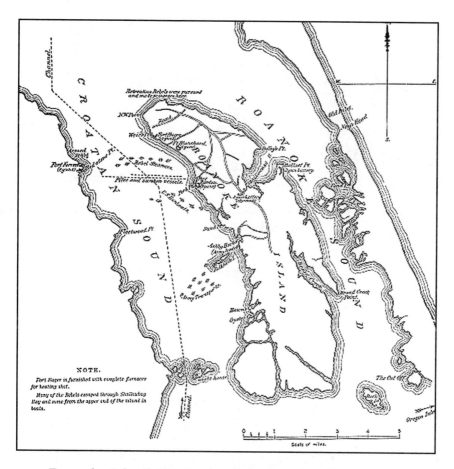

Roanoke Island, North Carolina, showing the position
of the Mosquito Fleet

Official Records Navy

The CSS *Alabama* sinks the USS *Hatteras* off the coast of Galveston, Texas, January 11, 1863

Semmes: *Memoirs of Service Afloat*

The CSS *Alabama* battles the USS *Kearsarge* off the coast of Cherbourg, France, June 19, 1864

Naval Historical Center

The CSS *Albemarle* rams and sinks the USS *Southfield*

The CSS *Albemarle* is rammed by the USS *Sassacus*

The CSS *Virginia* battles the USS *Monitor*, March 9, 1862

Naval Historical Center

Confederate ironclads, aground, and under fire at the Battle of Trent's Reach

Naval Historical Center

A bird's-eye view of the Battle of New Orleans

The CSS *Manassas* at the Battle of New Orleans

Battles and Leaders

The CSS *Arkansas* battles her way through the combined Federal fleets above Vicksburg

Naval Historical Center

The CSS *Chicora* and the CSS *Palmetto State* attack the Federal
blockaders off Charleston, January 31, 1863

Illustrated London News

The CSS *Tennessee* is pounded by Admiral Farragut's warships
at the Battle of Mobile Bay, August 5, 1864

Naval Historical Center

**Commander
John K. Mitchell**

Scharf: *History of the Confederate States Navy*

**Commander
William A. Webb,
captain of the
CSS *Atlanta***

Author's Collection

**Commander
James D. Johnston,
captain of the
CSS *Tennessee***

Naval Historical Center

Surgeon Daniel B. Conrad

He tended to the wounded
Admiral Buchanan on board the
CSS *Tennessee.*

Naval Historical Center

BIBLIOGRAPHY

———. *Civil War Naval Chronology*. Washington: Naval History Division, Navy Department, 1971.

———. *Official Records of the Union and Confederate Navies in the War of the Rebellion*. 31 volumes. Washington, D.C.: Government Printing Office, 1884–1927.

———. *The War of the Rebellion: A Compilation of the Official Records of the Union and Confederate Armies*. 130 volumes. Washington, D.C.: Government Printing Office, 1880–1901.

Brown, Isaac N. "The Confederate Gunboat *Arkansas*." *Battles and Leaders of the Civil War*. New York: The Century Company, 1884–1888.

Bulloch, James D. *The Secret Service of the Confederate States in Europe, or How the Confederate Cruisers Were Equipped*. 2 volumes. New York: Putnam Publishers, 1883.

Campbell, R. Thomas	*Academy on the James.* Shippensburg, Pa.: White Mane Publishing Company, Inc., 1998.
Campbell, R. Thomas	*The CSS H. L. Hunley.* Shippensburg, Pa.: White Mane Publishing Company, Inc., 1999.
Campbell, R. Thomas	*Fire and Thunder.* Shippensburg, Pa.: White Mane Publishing Company, Inc., 1997.
Campbell, R. Thomas	*Gray Thunder.* Shippensburg, Pa.: White Mane Publishing Company, Inc., 1996.
Campbell, R. Thomas	*Southern Fire.* Shippensburg, Pa.: White Mane Publishing Company, Inc., 1997.
Campbell, R. Thomas	*Southern Thunder.* Shippensburg, Pa.: White Mane Publishing Company, Inc., 1996.
Current, Richard N.	*Encyclopedia of the Confederacy.* 4 volumes. New York: Simon & Schuster, 1993.
Donnelly, Ralph W.	*The Rebel Leathernecks.* Shippensburg, Pa.: White Mane Publishing Company, Inc., 1989.
Luraghi, Raimondo	*History of the Confederate Navy.* Annapolis: Naval Institute Press, 1996.
Moebs, Thomas T.	*Confederate States Navy Research Guide.* Williamsburg, Va.: Moebs Publishing Company, 1991.
Scharf, J. Thomas	*History of the Confederate States Navy.* New York: Crown Publishers, Inc., 1877.

Semmes, Raphael   *Memoirs of Service Afloat.* Baltimore,
                           Md.: Kelly, Piet, 1869.

Stern, Philip Van Doren   *The Confederate Navy, A Pictorial His-
                           tory.* New York: Bonanza Books, 1962.

Still, William N.   *The Confederate Navy, The Ships, Men
                           and Organization, 1861–65.* Annapo-
                           lis, Md.: Naval Institute Press, 1997.

Wise, Stephen R.   *Lifeline of the Confederacy.* Columbia:
                           University of South Carolina Press,
                           1988.